The Sacred Mirror

The Sacred Mirror

Meeting God in Scripture

Herbert O'Driscoll

Anglican Book Centre
Toronto, Ontario

1984
Anglican Book Centre
600 Jarvis Street
Toronto, Ontario
M4Y 2J6

Cover design by
Saskia Walther

Typesetting by
Jay Tee Graphics Ltd.

Cover illustration: *Moses,*
by Pietro Annigoni; courtesy of
Miller Services

Printed in Canada

Canadian Cataloguing in Publication Data

O'Driscoll, Herbert.
The Sacred Mirror.
ISBN 0-919891-12-8
1. Meditations.   I. Title.
BV4832.2.037   1984   242   C83-099337-1

for Ted Scott,
archbishop and friend,
with respect and affection

Contents

The Sacred Mirror

All spirituality is founded on our human experience of being encountered by that which is Other than ourselves. From Abraham in Ur to Teresa in Calcutta, and in all the generations between their widely distanced centuries, countless men and women have testified to the God who has encountered their humanity.

There seems neither pattern of place nor limit to age in the ways the encounter takes place. It may be in childhood, in middle career, or in old age. It has been experienced in every conceivable circumstance, and in places as widely divergent as the bridge of a transatlantic slave ship (John Newton) and the upper seats of a London double-decker bus (C.S. Lewis). It has taken place with great emotion or with none, according to the temperament of the one involved. For a Christian the divine encounter will be a consciousness of being in the presence of Jesus Christ. The call to a certain course of action or to a certain way of life will be seen as his call.

In these pages I have taken some scripture passages that tell of certain moments when men and women knew they had encountered, and had been encountered by, that which was outside and above them, and was truly the Other. I have selected three different qualities of the eternal encounter. They are taken from what is sometimes called the old dispensation, before the birth of our Lord; from the fleeting years of his earthly ministry; and from the mysterious weeks when his risen Presence was still visible and tangible for the community struggling to birth after the traumatic events of his trial, crucifixion, and resurrection.

The encounter for Paul of Tarsus on the Damascus Road is told as a link between the New Testament community and all of us who have followed after. For Paul, as for us, the events of trial, suffering, resurrection, and ascension were already in the past. Yet into his life there came an encounter that made him realize his task was not a matter of eradicating the memory of

Jesus of Nazareth, but of coming to terms with the risen Christ as a contemporary who called him to a life-long service of such depth that it would become a joyful slavery.

Holy Scripture comes alive for us when we realize that it is about our lives. It is not of course about our lives only. It is about the life of God. But the great step of faith we dare to take is to affirm that there exists a love between Creator and creation, and that creation issues from the ceaselessly burning fire of that love. We affirm that God, having initiated creation, also sustains it by an indwelling Spirit. Finally there is the mystery of Incarnation, whereby we believe that the divine nature chose to enter creation in the form of our humanity, coming in ultimate humility as Mary's Child.

The story of all this is holy scripture. We believe that its insights have been passed down to us because men and women in other times realized that the events recorded, the lives described, the rich tapestry of human action and motivation woven, and, above all, the mysterious dialogue between God and our humanity that is expressed, are of timeless and universal significance. The voices of the scriptures, then, are our voices. Their agonies and joys speak to ours. Their faces uplifted to God are our faces. Thus scripture becomes a sacred mirror in which we see ourselves.

There is an old superstition about mirrors connected with All Hallows' Eve. It is said that on that night, if we look into a mirror, we will eventually see the features of our demon. I suspect that the old tale is based on a wise spiritual insight gained long before the word *psychology* had been invented. In the sacred mirror of the scriptures we do at times see demons. We learn that they reside in our human nature. But we see too the face whom Mother Julian of Norwich named our Maker, Lover, and Keeper. This is why I call these pages *The Sacred Mirror*. They are written out of my own looking into the mirror of scripture, in search not only of my own true face but of the face of our Lord.

Encountering Christ as a living contemporary Lord is the heart of Christian spirituality. When we read these particular encounters there remains for us a simple but important task. It is to discern where the scripture story can reflect our own lives. At the back of the book, by design, there are some blank pages for you to do this should you wish. Sometimes we may not so easily be able to see the face of Christ in experiences we have had. There may have been moments of grace received in many ways, terrible or beautiful. They may have come in the course of exercising our gifts or interests: art, music, travel, drama. They may have been in the mysterious country of our relationships. If in all these things there have been moments when we have become conscious of a Stranger walking with us, it may serve us well to write such moments down. When we do this, at least two things can happen. We may find that things hitherto unrealized in those experiences will be recognized. We may also find that the Stranger may cease to be such and may take on a surprising familiarity.

As we look into the mirror we may, like Mary of Magdala in the garden, and like John a few hundred yards from the lakeshore on a misty morning, find ourselves giving a cry of sudden and joyful recognition.

The Hidden One

The Desert

Now Moses was keeping the flock of his father-in-law, Jethro,
the priest of Mid'ian; and he led his flock to the west side of the
wilderness, and came to Horeb, the mountain of God. And the
angel of the Lord appeared to him in a flame of fire out of the
midst of a bush; and he looked, and lo, the bush was burning,
yet it was not consumed. And Moses said, "I will turn aside and
see this great sight, why the bush is not burnt." When the Lord
saw that he turned aside to see, God called to him out of the
bush, "Moses, Moses!" And he said, "Here am I." Then he said,
"Do not come near; put off your shoes from your feet, for the
place on which you are standing is holy ground." And he said,
"I am the God of your father, the God of Abraham, the God of
Isaac, and the God of Jacob." And Moses hid his face, for he
was afraid to look at God. Exodus 3:1–6

• • •

The encounter between Moses, one of the giants of human
history, and the God who called him on to the stage of that
history is given to us in particular detail. It is perhaps the
longest conversational exchange in the Bible, and one of the
most intriguing because of what it reveals about Moses.

When it takes place, it must seem to Moses as if the most
active part of his life is already over. The years in Egypt are
only a memory. So far as that great empire is concerned, he is a
convicted murderer and a traitor. He is now leading a largely
domestic existence. He is married, has a family, and is living
within an extended family or tribe. Every indication is that his
life will now pursue an uneventful course into his old age. For
Moses, however, as with Paul centuries later on the Damascus
Road, it is highly likely that the past is very much alive at
unconscious levels of his being. The memory, not just of the

particular injustice to a Hebrew slave, which made him kill, but of the continued oppression of his own people, is vivid and painful in the long silent hours as the flock moves across the semi-desert grazing grounds.

One day the burning within Moses burns in another way. At first what he sees looks perfectly normal, a sage bush suddenly igniting in the terrible heat of the noon sun. But this time it seems to blaze interminably. As he moves toward it, levels of his being that he had thought were left far behind in Egypt pour into his mind. Voices that had been silent are speaking — the soothing tones the princess he for so long called Mother, the harsh cry of a fellow Hebrew taunting him with the knowledge that Moses had already killed and hidden the body, the thin distant screams of someone feeling the daily lash in the Goshen mud flats. But through them all Moses becomes aware of another voice. It is quite different in quality. It sounds within and yet above the familiar voices. It speaks to his deepest being. He feels as if he is being physically forced to sink into the sand, to kick off the heavy sandals, to let the heat of the desert surge up through his skin. He feels every fibre of his being addressed. In his experience of the great gods of Egypt, looming in their splendid temples, he has never before felt the depth of awe now sweeping over him on this lonely barren mountain slope.

In the presence of a God greater than the gods, Moses crouches in supplication, hearing nothing but his own name echoing within him yet seeming to thunder across the steel vault of the desert sky. On and on it sounds, "Moses, Moses!" — not the screaming of any tyrant, only a terrible and quietly insistant majesty which he must respond to. Moses hears himself say, "Here am I," and in that very phrase he is conscious of knowing for the first time how he has come home to his ancient roots. He crouches, shaking in fear yet conscious of an immense peace. He knows himself to be a son of this God, to be one with the ancient fathers of this wandering wilderness, whose names had sounded distantly but now are pounding in the beating of his heart. "I am the God of your Father, the God of Abraham, the God of Isaac, and the God of Jacob." In the spare vivid words of the ancient story teller, "Moses hides his face, for he is afraid to look at God."

Who is not? Who would not be? To be other than afraid to look at God would be to reveal that we know neither ourselves nor God. We would be aware neither of our own finitude nor of God's infinity, neither of our own sinfulness nor of God's perfection. If our worshipping life is to have any vitality, it must bring us, even if only once in a lifetime, to a sense of presence that convicts us of this awesome gulf. There must come at least one touching of the bread to the hand, one flowing of the chaliced red wine to the lips, to convict us of the immeasurable cost by which this gulf has been crossed, and with what great love. Whether our desert place be a solitary room, a church pew, or a mountain top, a field, an ocean beach, or any other place of spiritual encounter, this we must seek, not obsessively but with the quiet certainty that it is for this encounter we are created. To kneel beside the burning bush, whenever or in whatever form it burns for us, is to find our most true selves, to come to our most true home. When we do so, one thing is certain. If that which we have encountered is true God, then we will not be allowed to dwell forever in the house to which we have come, even though it be truly ours; but we will be sent from it to do the will of him who brought us home.

So it was with Moses. The voice of God speaks of Egypt, distant in time and in miles. In Egypt there is a task to be completed. Moses is suddenly made aware that much of what has gone before is preparation for this task. This realization does not prevent his heart from convulsing with fear. For a convicted felon the return to Egypt will be a terrible risk. Apart from the risk there has already been too much wrenching pain, too much personal trauma and choice. For Moses, Egypt is a great wound, a scar in the mind not yet healed, and perhaps never to be healed. The very thought in the words "I will send you to Pharaoh" are enough to wring from him a denial of even the possibility. "Who am I that I should go to Pharaoh, and bring the sons of Israel out of Egypt?"

Immediately he is countered. There is a serene simplicity in the words. God says, "I will be with you." God says it to our humanity constantly. But we, as Moses, are not so easily assured. Trust comes uneasily to us. Much of our trust, so rich in childhood, becomes a casualty of our growing years. There have usually been too many betrayals received and given. Much of our inability to trust comes of our own guilt, the awareness that we ourselves have frequently not been found trustworthy.

Moses is not assured, but his instinct is to refrain from voicing his lack of trust. It is so with us in many conversations, particularly in interviews or in bargaining with others. We move off in another direction. We want an escape route, but it must be one other than confrontation and refusal, because we are guilty about these things. Moses goes, as we do, another way. Even as he moves toward it, we can feel the lack of conviction, the tentative sound that gives us all away when we are playing for time but are unwilling or unable to say simply No. It is the delaying tactic disguised as a request for more information.

"If . . . they ask me, 'What is his [God's] name?' what shall I say to them?" We can look at this moment, significant for Moses in his time, as also significant for us in ours. Long ago Egypt possessed a rich pantheon of gods. Anyone claiming a commission from a god had to name the god and give credentials for the task he was engaged in. Today, in a world of many authority sources, all paradoxically seeking authority in a society wary of any authority, we too have to name the basis on which we commend some policy or life style, some plan or order for society. When we ask the question, What is the theology of this? or What are the politics in this? we are asking the question that would have been shaped in long ago Egypt as What is the name of your god? In our Lord's lifetime, when he was asked, "By what authority do you do these things?" he too faced the same question.

The answer Moses gets is powerful and ultimate. "Say this to the people of Israel, 'I AM has sent me to you'." The reply resonates with life, energy, the pulse of existence. It expresses creativity, dynamism, all that exists, all that will be. It surrounds and subsumes all else. It is "the ground of our being," to use Tillich's great phrase. The answer goes far beyond Moses' pathetic self-serving question. When it describes the full scope of Moses' task, it crushes him even more. And finally it brings to the surface what is really at the heart of his problem: "They will not believe me or listen to my voice, for they will say, 'The Lord did not appear to you'." We can be certain that the emphasis is on that last word *you.*

We need to hear this moment in Moses' experience, because we share it. God may have called, touched, appeared to, spoken with other people. Perhaps God has come to the great saints, perhaps even to someone of particular sanctity whom we know, but surely never to *me*! God does not call people like me. I am ordinary and pedestrian. I have problems. I am not the stuff of encounter with God. So we all contend. It is essential to realize that every saint, every spiritual giant, once held this assumption. It is built into our humanity. It is the devil's last defence, so that even when we do feel called, Satan can rally us back to his side by our inability to think that we might be called, our fear lest we be regarded as crazy or pious or arrogant if we were to claim an encounter with God.

Almost with contempt God shows Moses certain signs of power that he already has. In what terms can we apply this divine reply to our own lives? God shows us abilities, gifts, experiences, that we have in abundance. These are richly endowed powers to face our Pharaohs. But in this wonderful and maddening essay on our humanity, Moses still remains unconvinced. He retreats one more time. We can detect a note of anxiety. He knows he is testing the divine patience! "Oh, my Lord, I am not eloquent. I am slow of speech and of tongue." The reply reveals that the divine patience is tested! The plea is brushed aside. What we communicate is not by eloquence so much as by the reality of who we are. Eloquence without such reality is eventually ineffective. "I will be with your mouth, and teach you what you shall speak." But Moses is still not satisfied and again protests. It would later be said that "the Lord used to speak to Moses face to face, as a man speaks to his friend." This moment is the first great testing of that friendship. There is a face to face quality about this moment. "The anger of the Lord was kindled against Moses and he said, 'Is there not Aaron, your brother, the Levite? I know that he can speak well!' "

At last Moses is silent. It is interesting what has silenced him. He is to be given a companion, a brother. How interesting that the Christian gospel, as it calls for our sometimes fearful and pathetic allegiance, does not offer us a grace of some intangible kind, but rather a flesh and blood Lord. And further, is it not salutary that more and more twentieth-century Christians are realizing that this same Lord touches us in those physical and tangible hands which, in the name of Jesus Christ, touch us daily, disguised as familiar, or sometimes even unfamiliar, people.

In the introduction of Aaron we see another significant thing. In countless tasks we have found how the feat that limits us in offering our gifts is dealt with by someone else offering precisely the gifts we may lack. That person is our "Aaron." With that person, and with others in a Christian community of mingled weaknesses and strengths, we can lead both ourselves and others out of many slaveries, many prisons, many exiles, bringing both ourselves and them to a new quality of life and fulfilment and creativity.

The Mountain

Jez'ebel sent a messenger to Eli'jah, saying, "So may the gods do
to me, and more also, if I do not make your life as the life of one
of them by this time tomorrow." Then he was afraid, and he
arose and went for his life, and came to Beer-sheba, which
belongs to Judah, and left his servant there. And there he came
to a cave, and lodged there; and behold, the word of the Lord
came to him, and he said to him, "What are you doing here,
Eli'-jah?" He said, "I have been very jealous for the Lord, the
God of hosts; for the people of Israel have forsaken thy cove-
nant, thrown down thy altars, and slain thy prophets with the
sword; and I, even I only, am left; and they seek my life, to
take it away." And he said, "Go forth, and stand upon the
mount before the Lord." And behold, the Lord passed by, and
a great and strong wind rent the mountains, and broke in
pieces the rocks before the Lord, but the Lord was not in the
wind; and after the wind an earthquake, but the Lord was not
in the earthquake; and after the earthquake a fire, but the Lord
was not in the fire; and after the fire a still small voice. 1 Kings
19:2, 3, 9–12

• • •

In the myth of Parsifal there comes a moment when the young
knight is being welcomed and feted in Arthur's court at
Camelot. His deeds have earned him universal praise, and this
he is being given. At the height of the celebration there enters a
hideous old woman. Silencing the court she proceeds to enum-
erate every conceivable fault, weakness, and error that can
possibly be connected with Parsifal. By the end of her recital
she has reduced the proud young knight to a pathetic figure
shorn of honour and self-esteem. Jungian psychology sees in
this mythical event, the playing out of a moment that fre-

quently occurs in a man's life. At the culmination of worldly
achievement there arises from his deepest self what Jung calls
the *Anima*. This force, coming from the feminine side of his
nature, attacks the very foundation of his achievement and
sometimes demolishes both it and him, making him regard all
that has been achieved as meaningless and reducing him to
despair.

By the middle of the tenth century B.C. the kingdom so
painstakingly fashioned by David the King had broken into
two marginally viable monarchies named Israel and Judah.
While they indulged their petty jealousies of one another, the
overall quality of their institutional and political morality
declined. Both became more and more embroiled in the cynical
and eventually fatal machinations of international power
politics played out around them by great empires. Through all
of this, holy scripture orchestrates a deeper and more
mysterious theme of religious conflict. The writer of the Book
of Kings would say that this level of conflict was the ultimate
issue at stake, and that all other struggle and tragedy issued
from this. We might frame the question being asked in this
period, "How is reality to be seen"? But they asked it in terms of
"What God is to be served"?

The issue was a very real one. It had to do with the realities
of power, violence, armies, coups, palace intrigue. The whole
moral and social ordering of Israel was at stake. Men and
women saw themselves as struggling under conflicting
allegiances either to Jehovah, the God who had long called
Israel and Judah to a high morality and a progressive history,
or to Baal, the nature god who called men and women to the
sun and the moon, the seeding and the harvest, the round of
the earth's seasons, the recurrence of the menstrual cycle — a
universe of cyclic repetition, predictability, passivity, sen-
suality.

We enter this history at the supreme moment of confrontation in this tiny strife torn society. Ahab the King has married a
Phoenician princess named Jezebel. She has brought with her

from Tyre an army of priests of Baal, courtiers who are efficiently infiltrating all public life preparatory to taking over power in Israel. Heading the forces of reaction to this foreign cult is the prophet or moral leader named Elijah. He is convinced that, if he does not act quickly, the slide into moral degeneracy and political takeover will be irreversible. In desperation he risks his life in a dramatic public confrontation with Jezebel's henchmen. Meeting on Mount Carmel, against the backdrop of the Mediterranean to the west and the verdant valley of Jezreel to the east, Elijah engineers a symbolic contest of the Gods, Baal and Jehovah. He emerges victor, and the result is the slaughter of hundreds of the priests of Baal.

It is Elijah's supreme moment. He has achieved his objective. In an ecstasy of victorious celebration he runs before Ahab's chariot all the way east to Jezreel, the king's winter palace. It is at this precise moment when he is overcome by a dreadful wave of depression. In all literature no more vivid portrait exists of this common human experience. It begins not with something imagined but with a grim reality. Elijah does not make the mistake of dismissing Jezebel merely because she is a woman. He realizes that she wields real and vicious power that is all the more dangerous because it has suffered a setback. He decides to avoid capture. Turning away he disappears into the terrible emptiness stretching south and west of the desert outpost of Beersheba.

As for Elijah, so for us all — it can sometimes be wise to seek refuge, to refuse to face something that we know has the capacity to destroy us. Wisdom tells us we should confront reality. It does not, we might note, tell us when we should do so. It may well be that now is not the time to stand and do battle with what eventually has to be faced, whether it be a necessary clash in relationships or a confrontation in business or professional life. It may be more important first to withdraw for the express purpose of gaining strength to deal with the situation effectively. To do battle in exhaustion is foolish. To underestimate the forces against one can be disastrous. Elijah "was afraid, and he arose and went for his life, and came to Beer-sheba." It was a wise decision.

At such times there is always another choice to be made. When should we turn to friends, and when should we seek solitariness? A good rule of thumb is first to seek friends for reflection and then solitariness for decision. It seems as if solitariness consciously chosen allows us to encounter our deepest self and to face our most genuine motivations. Thus "Elijah came to Beersheba . . . and left his servant there. But he himself went a days journey into the wilderness." Solitariness consciously chosen can be rich precisely because it is costly. There follow for Elijah nights and days that merge into one another. Weariness and depression fashion a strange world where dream and actuality are interwoven, in which a demoralized fugitive is fed by those whom his delirium remembers as angels. Long afterwords he will recall only the wish to die, that all too familiar companion of prolonged depression, the desperate weariness of body and soul that shrieks against even one more task, one more responsibility, one more pressure.

Time passes. The wanderer begins to recover a sense of awareness. With it comes to him, as to us all, the pain of emotion returning with the recovery of physical strength. He moves beyond mere instinctive revival to emotional awareness. As he moves deeper into the terrible wilderness of sand and rock, Elijah encounters a like emptiness in the wilderness of his own interior landscape. The choosing of solitariness does not yield its rewards easily or early, as we commit ourselves to it. Slowly realization comes. He has fled the scene of his greatest triumph. By doing so he has probably lost any vestige of advantage he may have gained. Guilt, another familiar offspring of depression, grips him. He agonizes, "I am no better than my fathers," and from that precarious ledge of self condemnation he topples into the gulf of potential suicide, "Lord, take away my life."

Sleep, stillness, the instinctive urge to survive, to reach the destination that calls him, the unquenchable conviction that God *is* even when God seems to be absent, all make it possible for Elijah to penetrate to the heart of the wilderness. The pattern is testified to in countless spiritual journeys. God does not dwell on the outer fringes of the desert. Only to those who push on to the heart of the wilderness does the prospect of the sacred mountain appear. "Elijah arose, and ate and drank, and went in the strength of that food . . . to Horeb (Sinai) the mount of God." In the desert of despair, of sorrow, of suffering, there are those who have reached for the sacred food and drink, finding it dry and tasteless for many days. Yet, as they faithfully continue to reach toward it, they begin to taste a bread that is more than bread, a wine that is more than wine, until nourished and newly energized they are enabled to approach the mountain of God, beautiful and terrible in the desert yet soaring above it.

On Sinai Elijah seeks and finds refuge. He enters a cave, instinctively burying himself in the stone womb of the mountain as he seeks rebirth. Such, if we are wise, is our purpose in seeking refuge. We speak of "burying" ourselves in a book, a hobby, a task. We speak wisely if it means that we are, by the same act, waiting for new birth.

There now comes to Elijah the salient question we all face at some moment. "What are you doing here, Elijah"? The question has all the therapeutic power of the most enlightened psychological insight. It is the key that opens the door of Elijah's agony, letting it all spill out. "I have been very jealous for the Lord, the God of hosts," he claims. It is a cry of self-justification. "The people of Israel have forsaken thy covenant, thrown down thy alters, and slain thy prophets with the sword; and I, even I only, am left." The shriek of wholesale condemnation is mingled with resentment. For Elijah all Israel has become a "they" meriting only contempt. In this we hear the voice of paranoia. It is the same "they" encountered in the depressions of all our lives. In the face of those dark legions of lonely alienation, we have all cried out with Elijah, "I, even I only, am left." I am the only conscientious member of the firm. I am the only genuinely devout person in this fellowship. I am the only one who knows what God wants in this or that matter. Everyone else is against me. Thus Elijah cries out, "They seek my life, to take it away."

The reply of God is magnificently orchestrated. Elijah is commanded to "go forth and stand upon the mount before the Lord." The first basic response he must make is to leave the cave. That is demanded of all of us. The cave is not an unhealthy element in life, so long as we occupy it only long enough for regeneration to begin. But then it is essential that we make the effort to emerge "before the Lord." Having emerged we can begin the second stage of recovery. The mere fact that we are expecting to be shown the grace of God helps us to discern the presence of God.

Now through Elijah's experience we are given a warning about the sometimes paradoxical ways of God. Elijah and we learn that God does not chose melodrama as a mode of entry. "A great and strong wind rent the mountains, . . . but the Lord was not in the wind; and after the wind an earthquake, but the Lord was not in the earthquake; and after the earthquake a fire, but the Lord was not in the fire." The repeated absence of God is from the larger-than-life moment, the dramatic, the exotic. When we ourselves are in a heightened state of perception, as we sometimes are in sorrow, in tension, in crisis, we seek God's presence in the heightened and the para-normal. It seems necessary to our own emotional exaltation. But "after the fire a still small voice." The lesson is taught us again and again, and we forget it again and again. The presence of God is a deceptively clothed glory. It chooses simplicity. So intently do we seek it in the magnificent and the awesome, that we pass it by in the ordinary. "I come," says the God of Evelyn Underhill, "in the little things."

Also the question, now once more repeated, is deceptively simple. "What are you doing here, Elijah?" Its profundity lies in the recognition that the poison of self-pity and self-justification, resentment and fear, is still residually preventing Elijah's recovery. There is more of it to be drawn out. Frequently, when as well-meaning friends we try to help, we often presume that the particular problem is fully dealt with at an early stage. We do this because there is a natural tendency to move as quickly as possible through the unpleasant to the joyful, to presume that the "dying" elements in the situation are fully dealt with and the process of "resurrection" is already begun. The experience of Elijah suggests that it may be necessary to ask the unwelcome, probing, even annoying questions again and again.

Elijah's reply reveals that little has changed. Scripture is never facile. The encounter with God does not necessarily have a magic effect. Elijah is anything but transformed. The whole sequence of depression is poured out, resentment, alienation, paranoia. Everyone seeks to do him harm. Life itself is still the enemy. Now we begin to see the real effect of the whole process Elijah has gone through. The last outburst has cleansed him. The journey inward is ended; the turning outward has begun. He begins to think again, to plan again, to act again. "Return to the wilderness of Damascus; . . . Anoint Hazeal to be king over Syria; . . . Jehu . . . king over Israel." Chilling in its implication is the third order. "Elisha . . . you shall anoint to be prophet in your place."

When the future is seen in specifics, however formidable, it becomes possible to set about responding. But what doubly ensures the possibility of response is Elijah's realizing that there are "seven thousand in Israel, all the knees that have not bowed to Baal, and every mouth that has not kissed him." Elijah realizes that it is simply not true that life itself is the enemy, that all seek his life. Some do. There is always someone who dislikes us, seeks to discredit us, even sometimes to do us harm. Among all the imagined threats that would immobilize us, there is an element of reality. The moment the imagined legions are recognized for the unreality they are, then the real can be faced.

The simple realization that we are not alone can in itself be immensely energizing to the human spirit. The knowledge that a community exists and can be found, even if it is not available at the present moment, can be sufficient to motivate our journey toward it. To encounter it is to be empowered to serve the God who in Christ called into being the Christian community.

The Temple

In the year that King Uzzi'ah died I saw the Lord sitting upon a throne, high and lifted up; and his train filled the temple. Above him stood the seraphim; each had six wings: with two he covered his face, and with two he covered his feet, and with two he flew. And one called to another and said: "Holy, holy, holy is the Lord of hosts; the whole earth is full of his glory." And the foundations of the thresholds shook at the voice of him who called, and the house was filled with smoke. And I said: "Woe is me! For I am lost; for I am a man of unclean lips, and I dwell in the midst of a people of unclean lips; for my eyes have seen the King, the Lord of hosts!" Then flew one of the seraphim to me, having in his hand a burning coal which he had taken with tongs from the altar. And he touched my mouth, and said: "Behold, this has touched your lips; your guilt is taken away, and your sin forgiven." And I heard the voice of the Lord saying, "Whom shall I send, and who will go for us?" Then I said, "Here am I! Send me." Isaiah 6:1-8

• • •

As the young man walked in the temple area, his mind was in turmoil. It was not that his position in the regime was insecure. For some time he had played a reasonably prominent part in the affairs of the country. But for any man in public life, a change of government always brings questions, doubts, a certain anxiety.

The kingdom of Judah was in reasonably good shape. The years of Uzziah as king had been good. There had been a deal of war, but it had not been for the sake of aggrandizement. Uzziah had merely taken care to show that Judah was capable of defending herself if she had to. The military had never become an obsession with him. If anything, he had concentrated on agriculture, and that had been very necessary in a country whose climate always placed it on a knife edge between plenty and famine. Now Uzziah was dead and Jothan was on the throne. In reality Jothan had been ruler for some years, because of his father's illness. The young man reflecting in the temple suddenly realized ruefully that he and the new king were about the same age. He smiled as he realized that it made him feel old to be the king's contemporary.

But there were more distant things to be concerned about, things that could yet threaten them all. Something huge was happening to the north east, greater and of more consequence than anything in their history. Only three years ago a new name had begun to be talked about along the northern caravan routes, the name of a Persian called Tigleth Pilesar. "Pul" they said for short. Already his armies had marched across the top of the eastern world and gone as far as the Aegean. They were now pushing toward Damascus and down the coast. The young statesman knew that it was only a matter of time before this small and prosperous state would be probed by a growing empire flexing its military muscle. As the young man thought of those marching hordes, he had a vision of them ringing Jerusalem, and he feared for his wife and two small sons.

The young man's name was Isaiah. He was now twenty-five years old, able, prominent, publicly involved, and yet, in some way he found difficult to explain, ambivalent about himself, his society, and his role in it. That day in 742 BC in the temple area, he was about to experience a presence which, by its demands upon him, would change and shape his life and his work until he died. Years later he tried to describe the shattering experience which turned a public servant into a prophet and inspired in him some of the most sublime utterances the world would ever hear. That same vision, in which Isaiah would encounter the presence of the living God, would stand as the classic pattern for the way in which men and women in every century would encounter the timeless call of that same Lord.

Isaiah begins the central element of his personal story in a very instinctive and human way. As with all of us describing a life-changing moment, he sets the time of the experience as precisely as possible. "In the year that King Uzziah died," he says, "I saw the Lord." Here Isaiah evokes two images that are full of meaning for us who read them in this late twentieth century. We live in an age when the "king" is dying, if by the concept *King*, we mean the hitherto authoritative structures of society as we have known them. If institutions, customs, traditions, organizations, economic and political systems are kings, then, in the sense that all are changing, all are to some extent dying. Viewed in this way our age has about it a great deal of turmoil and terror.

Yet, like Isaiah, we are faced with a strange almost paradoxical fact. It is precisely in this age of dying kings that millions of people are "seeing the Lord." Millions are finding themselves aware of a new and vibrant spiritual dimension in their lives. Millions are finding themselves called to an allegiance they would once have never considered. "High and lifted up" is the phrase Isaiah used. It describes much contemporary spirituality. It is a heightening of our perception of the sacred. For millions of Christians the main elements of faith, both sacrament and word, have attained a high and intense level of significance.

"His train filled the temple . . . . the whole earth is full of his glory." In Isaiah's consciousness image and heavenly song swirl and mingle, reflecting the totality of God's presence. Isaiah sees that God is everywhere. Religious consciousness today is gaining this same vision. There is a growing awareness of the sacred nature of creation itself, a realizing that all contemporary questions are essentially spiritual questions. Our explorations into space, into biology, into the extension or abortion of human life, our capability to destroy the human environment, either gradually by excessive exploitation or instantaneously by nuclear holocaust — all are questions of immense spiritual significance.

The seraphim "had six wings: . . . with two he flew." For Isaiah the sacred objects of his cultic experience, the temple figures, are no longer fixed as they had been in reality. In his vision they have taken flight. But his experience is precisely ours. The "fixed" points in our experience are no longer fixed. Society, relationships, customs, traditions, assumptions, moralities — all are in motion. They have become protean, malleable, mobile, unpredictable.

"The foundations . . . shook at the voice of him who called, and the house was filled with smoke." Isaiah's world was shaking, but the very shaking had at its heart a voice, a meaning. The shaking was not merely chaotic but calling. There was for Isaiah, and there is for us today, a mingling of terrors and a haunting call for response in the midst of terror. The image of smoke is itself ambiguous. Smoke can bring confusion, lostness, fear. It can also evoke, in the form of incense, the timeless symbol of the presence of the Holy.

We see the humanity of Isaiah's response. Confronted with the presence of God, and aware that the same God is somehow asking for response, Isaiah is overcome by a sense of appalled inadequacy. Insecurity and self doubt, latent in us all, wells up in him. It is impossible that he can be of use to God's purposes. This is his first reaction. Not only Isaiah but we too feel ourselves tainted and contaminated, both by our personal weakness and by the shortcomings of society, with all its compromises and ambiguities. Not only have we "unclean lips," but we feel that "we dwell in the midst of a people of unclean lips." Yet even here we cannot escape the call. Our late twentieth century eyes have, in a spiritual sense, caught a glimpse of the Lord on the awesome canvas of our present history. Our "eyes have seen the King."

At this moment in Isaiah's vision comes the divine initiative that is so mysterious yet familiar in our own experience. Our human instinct to retreat from God's call, our human inability to respond, is met, not with a corresponding retreat on God's part but with an offer of grace. "Then flew one of the seraphim

to me, having in his hand a burning coal . . . from the altar.
And he touched my mouth."

With the gesture, accompanied by images of warmth, fire,
concern, touch, comes the assurance each of us needs and
longs so much to hear. "Guilt is taken away . . . sin forgiven."
Only when given that inner freedom from the chains of guilt
and lack of self-worth that rattle away in the dungeons of our
subconscious being — only then can we really hear the call of
God to a particular action and responsibility. "I heard the voice
of the Lord," cries Isaiah. What the Lord is asking is no longer
traumatizing, even though the divine call can never be heard
by any of us with less than awe. "Whom shall I send?" is that
call. And we, if we have been released by grace to do so,
answer, "Here am I! Send me."

Very often we are impoverished by an inability to recognize
what is, for Isaiah in his vision, a burning coal from the altar.
We fail to recognize the means of grace, partly because we in
the western world are chronically given to limiting the divine
approach only to stated religious categories. We look for
grace, a word we almost always link with religion, only in offi-
cially religious channels, while grace flows through and
around us in a thousand disguises in what we ironically call
"natural" ways. Grace may well be a letter received, a gift
given, a phone call, a casual conversation, a new relationship,
an insight, a book read, a work of art seen in a new way, a
touch of hands, a restoring medication, an understanding of
something for the first time, a good night's sleep, a making
love, a Eucharist — on and on can go the list of possibilities of
grace so easily unrecognized.

We live in a world of sometimes brutal realism. The
response of Isaiah is met by his receiving a chilling responsibility. He is to speak for God to a people who will at best
answer grudgingly and at worst be totally incapable of even
hearing. This is followed by an even grimmer prospect. He
himself, obviously sobered by the terms of what he is called to,
asks despairingly, "How long, O Lord"?

The reply is in terms that we in this late century of considerable dread can recognize all too easily. The very opening phrase of the passage, "Until cities lie waste without inhabitant," is an image we have seen as fact since the mushroom clouds over Hiroshima. We have seen lands "utterly desolate," whether they be created deserts by nuclear experimentation or by vast migration in areas such as the Sahel. In many great cities we have seen whole blighted blocks of "houses without men." In our struggle with migration because of war or economic crisis, we are familiar with the reality of the phrase, "The Lord removes men far away."

In all this grim contemporary context our capacity to respond to God's call is often tested to the core. Yet even to Isaiah there is an opening given in the dark portrait of the future. He is placed on a plain of desperation — the context we know to be so easily possible for our own civilization, unless we are capable of great changes of attitude in international relationships. On this plain there stands a tree. It is broken and blasted by all that has taken place, yet it still contains seed, the seed of the future.

Here, in classic Biblical fashion, is the image of a hope that is unquenchable. This hope, for Isaiah and for us, becomes the source of grace. It becomes the burning coal from the altar of the future, which touches us and releases us from immobilizing fear and hopelessness. As we look through Isaiah's vision at the blackened tree stump in the desert of a possible future, it becomes before our eyes another tree. It still images death, with its limbs in the form of a cross, yet to us who are signed with that same cross, it becomes also a symbol of potential resurrection.

The Valley

The hand of the Lord was upon me, and he brought me out by the Spirit of the Lord, and set me down in the midst of the valley; it was full of bones. And he led me round among them; and behold, there were very many upon the valley; and lo, they were very dry. And he said to me, "Son of man, can these bones live?" And I answered, "O Lord God, thou knowest." Again he said to me, "Prophesy to these bones, and say to them, O dry bones, hear the word of the Lord. Thus says the Lord God to these bones: Behold, I will cause breath to enter you, and you shall live. And I will lay sinews upon you, and will cause flesh to come upon you, and cover you with skin, and put breath in you, and you shall live; and you shall know that I am the Lord." So I prophesied as he commanded me, and the breath came into them, and they lived, and stood upon their feet, an exceedingly great host. Ezekiel 37:1-6, 10

• • •

On a certain day in the year 586 BC an onlooker from the mountain top to the east of Jerusalem, a slope later to be called the Mount of Olives, would have seen the destruction of a society. It was not a holocaust in the sense of human slaughter, though many died. It was a concerted effort, by a huge invading force, to raze the walled city. Amid the destruction thousands of citizens were being formed into groups and readied for the long march into the great empire to the east. The onlooker would have been witness to the execution of a political decision by Nebuchadnezzar, the ruler of the Babylonian empire. It was a decision to eradicate the tiny state that lay between his domain and the approach to the edge of Egypt. Jerusalem as a city was to be destroyed. Those who enabled the small nation to function — its professionals, its artists, its politicians, its business class — were to be brought in exile to the homelands of the empire. On that particular day these operations were being carried out with efficiency, dispatch, and brutality.

Among the exiles outside the burning walls that day, there would have been a young man whose name was Ezekial. He was to play a key role in the preservation of morale among his people. Over the next half century the experience of that people was not entirely to be one of victimization. They possessed a great advantage by having in common with Babylonian commercial life the eastern language called Aramaic. Many Jews prospered. Many became influential in Babylonian society. But for many others exile remained an agony. That agony was expressed in various ways. Its hatred and resentment remains vivid and haunting in the words of a song sung by a poet of that time. We possess it in the Bible as Psalm 137.

> By the waters of Babylon,
> there we sat down and wept,
> when we remembered Zion.
> O daughter of Babylon, you devastator!
> Happy shall he be who requites you
> with what you have done to us!
> Happy shall he be who takes your little ones
> and dashes them against the rock!

But such romantic melancholy was not chosen by all the exiles. Some saw that, while plaintive song relieved the emotions, it did not motivate the heart or strengthen the will. This task was to engage the extraordinary man we have already met among the prisoners taken to Babylon. We possess a great deal of what he said. We know that he had a magnificent gift for images that communicated with power and great clarity. But of all his communications to his people, nothing had such devastating effect as his image of the valley of bones. It remains forever as one of the world's great universal images, its ingredients applicable again and again to the human situation.

As Ezekial moves into his vision there is no doubt about the divine initiative. Ezekial is not choosing; he is being chosen. In the words of an old Kalahari Desert bush man, spoken in this century to Laurens Van Der Post, the prophet feels that he is "A Dream that someone is Dreaming." Ezekial says of this moment, "The hand of the Lord was upon me, and he brought me out by the Spirit of the Lord, and set me down in the midst of the valley."

In a post Freudian world it is interesting to consider the one thing all twentieth-century psychologies have in common: their suggestion that to be human is to be driven by some particular element in our being. Opinions differ as to which is the ultimate motivating element. For Freud it is our sexuality, for Jung it is our urge for wholeness, for Frankl it is our search for meaning. There is no reason to deny any of these as being motivating sources of our behaviour and deciding. For a Judeo-Christian man or woman, however, the definition of source would go one step further. It would move to the intuition that, however powerful these channels of our motivation are, the ultimate source is the mystery we would variously called God, Christ, Holy Spirit. For us, for Ezekial, the hand upon us is that of the Lord; the spirit we perceive is that of the Lord. If in our lives we are set down in certain valleys of experience, it is in some way, not always easy to understand or accept, the Lord who sets us in them. Here we are touching on one of the impenetrable mysteries of human existence, but many would say that such an outlook at least makes it possible to seek some meaning for the "valley" which sometimes threatens to overwhelm us.

In Ezekial's vision there is no gradual revealing of the situation, no easy approach. The valley, we are told, was "full of bones." The language is short, monosyllabic. It drops us into nothing, like the broken string on an instrument. Here there are no colors to engage the eye. There is only one terrible thing — death.

When is utter truth, utter realism, therapeutic? When is it wise to face something totally head on? Sometimes a doctor must decide to be frank in telling bad news. There are those of us who can be devastated by this approach, and those who are galvanized into activity and creativity by it. A recent book by Jonathan Schell, *The Fate of the Earth*, draws a horrifyingly graphic account of a twenty megaton explosive device being detonated above Manhattan. He does this and more on the grounds that an utterly detailed and specific acquaintance with the possibilities of the present nuclear confrontation can be in itself therapeutic. It can send us into creative response rather than traumatizing us into immobility.

For the prophet there is at least an initial period of trauma. He dwells on the image of bones, repeating it as if he cannot yet believe the immensity of death around him. "He [the Lord] led me round among them; and behold, there were very many upon the valley; and lo, they were very dry." The prospect is appalling. To return to the nuclear realities of our own day — we can identify with Ezekial if we think of those moments when we see listed or pictured in some way the full extent of destruction held within the armories of the world at this time. Numbers confront us, financial and technological, which numb the mind.

As to Ezekiel so to us there comes the terrifying question, wrung from us in our trauma. "Can these bones live?" We ask it of the "desert" features of our own experience, asking it of our deepest selves. Have I got the energy, psychic or physical, to pull out of this experience? Can I survive this sorrow? Can I function much longer under this daily pressure? Am I ever going to emerge from this depression? These are the questions we ask of our internal world. We also ask such questions of external things. Can the institutional church really be a creative element at a serious level in our own society? Can our institutions weather this period of great testing? Can society survive? Can the race survive its own capacity for self destruction? Not one of us is stranger to these questions. Ezekial speaks for every man and woman when he hears the voice of

God within him asking the terrible question, "Can these bones live?"

It is typical of the power and honesty of the vision that there is no confident answer on the lips of a suddenly heroic prophet. The answer he does give is magnificent. Ezekial says, "O Lord God, thou knowest," but it is by implication an admission of human fallibility and even doubt. Ezekial is also saying, "I simply don't know. The prospect is so terrible I have to be open to the possibility that I am looking at a dreadful finality." To say this is to do no more than describe a perfectly defensible contemporary stance. To take it is not to betray faith. Any faith today that has not felt itself forced into silence by the facts of the human situation, is not worthy of the name. Real faith exists, and must always exist, in a context of potential doubt.

What Ezekial does say is very different from a mere "I don't know." He says, "O Lord God, thou knowest." This is the attitude faith calls us to today. We face the evidence that must be faced. There is no head-burying in the sand; such is a travesty of faith as well as a shirking of reality. All we can claim is a humble yet profound certainty that there is One who knows, One in whom ultimate meaning resides and from whom it issues.

There now comes a command to Ezekial that he prophesy. On the surface this seems the height of futility. "Prophesy to these bones," is the command. It seems an insult to human intelligence. Yet many today have heard the same command. Millions of people, fully aware of the world's skeletal poverty in many senses, have quietly decided to give themselves to a hope that has been lit within them. In churches and voluntary organizations, in trades and professions, in politics, in media, in art, in every human endeavor, they have decided by choosing hope to prophesy to the bones of the present world.

What these people are saying, though they may use thought and planning and action more than words, is what the voice of God says to Ezekial. It is the promise of hope: "I will cause breath to enter you, and you shall live. And I will lay sinews upon you, and will cause flesh to come upon you, and cover you with skin . . . and you will know that I am the Lord." The voice of God says to him and to us that the ingredient we bring to the future, the one element that we can give to the building blocks of the future, is precisely our willingness to respond, to give ourselves to the "desert," to prophesy even if bones are the only audience. Given our human faithfulness God can form the future, a future that is both human and divine in its sources, its energy, its creativity.

In response to the prophet's faithful human response "the bones came together, bone to its bone." Is there a hint in this part of the vision that the first step in new life and new faith is a gathering into community? There follows in the vision the coming of sinews, flesh, skin. Does community furnish a basic framework upon which new life can be built? Can the community, by drawing upon each member's gifts, give back to each member a revitalizing strength?

But the physical elements of recovery, whether they be numbers or energy or power, whether in things religious or social or political, are not themselves what the Lord of history seeks. There still remains, as in Ezekial's vision, the need for the "breath," the Spirit of God, to enter into the human process of recovery. Without that breath the physical is merely that and no more. In the moment of the formation of our humanity in Genesis, it is the breath of God upon the dust that creates. Before that breathing, our dust had human form but not yet human reality. In Ezekial's vision, before a great army could form, bone and sinew, flesh and skin had to be animated by the breath of God. The human predicament today, occupying its valley of mingled dread and hope, possesses a future to the degree that we can open the bones of our humanity, personal and social, institutional and political, to the revitalizing breath of the God of history.

The Incarnate One

A Strength of Age

Now there was a man in Jerusalem, whose name was Simeon, and this man was righteous and devout, looking for the consolation of Israel, and the Holy Spirit was upon him. And it had been revealed to him by the Holy Spirit that he should not see death before he had seen the Lord's Christ. And inspired by the Spirit he came into the temple; and when the parents brought in the child Jesus, to do for him according to the custom of the law, he took him up in his arms and blessed God. And there was a prophetess, Anna, the daughter of Phanuel, of the tribe of Asher; she was of a great age, having lived with her husband seven years from her viginity, and as a widow till she was eighty-four. She did not depart from the temple, worshipping with fasting and prayer night and day. And coming up at that very hour she gave thanks to God, and spoke of him to all who were looking for the redemption of Jerusalem. Luke 2:25-28, 36-38

• • •

But for Luke we would have hardly a glimpse of the childhood of our Lord. From Mark we have nothing. In his gospel we meet Jesus at the age of approximately thirty, about to begin his public ministry. John in his gospel does speak of nativity, but it is indirectly expressed. In effect he sings a great song or anthem as prelude to his book, telling of the enfleshing of the eternal Word so that humanity may see "his glory." Even in John's first chapter we move after a few opening verses to the coming of John the Baptist and, therefore, to the emergence of our Lord as adult.

We will never know exactly why Luke chose to include the magnificent and lyrical story that fills his first two chapters. We merely thank God he did! We cannot help wonder at the intriguing possibilities of their source. Did he at some stage in his gathering of material make contact with the now aging woman who remembered the vivid moments of her son's childhood? Was there a gentle but pointed questioning, a hasty scribbling to catch a particular nuance or phrase? Were there attempts, probing but judicious, interposed in the conversation, to jog her aging memory?

The incident happens in the temple immediately after Mary receives the baby back from the trembling hands of the old man Simeon. As a young mother she is nervous about her child. Being in the temple was in itself nerve-racking for two rural people, strangers to the south and to the shrieking bustling streets of Jerusalem. To be faced suddenly with the elderly Simeon — his obvious ecstatic interest in the child making him oblivious of gathering public attention, his cryptic and terrible image of a sword piercing her heart — was almost too much for the young mother to bear. She may well have longed desperately for a way of escape from what has suddenly become public spectacle and private agony.

At this very moment in our concern for Mary, Luke introduces Anna. That she should be introduced at all is intriguing. If, as he writes this temple episode, Luke's purpose is to link the birth of Jesus to the ancient tradition of prophecy, he has already achieved this through the person of Simeon. Why introduce a second link and, particularly, why a woman? Far from supposing that a woman should not be introduced, we are trying to suggest that there must have been some special reason for Luke's including the elderly Anna. If we allow the possibility that Luke based this episode on the recollections of Mary, then it may well be that, because Anna's femininity gave assurance and support to the younger woman, her presence was too significant for Luke to do anything else but include.

Luke says that Anna "was of a great age, having lived with her husband seven years from her virginity and as a widow till she was eighty-four." For some reason Luke is at pains to emphasize her age. It may of course be sheer admiration. In that generation eighty-four was a prodigious age to achieve.

But Luke goes further. There is the precision about her life experience. He tells us that for a few short years there had been a marriage, long ago. For seven years Anna had presumably known love; for over seventy she had known, if not loneliness, at least solitude. One asks the reason for Luke's seeming precision. Why does he mention at all that long-gone treasured virginity given in the passion of an early marriage?

Is there here an example of Luke's great sensitivity? Is a consummate writer responding to the subtle ironies that give drama to human life. Is Luke portrait painting, highlighting similarities and contrasts, subtly working with the lightest brush strokes on the canvas of our minds. The faces of the two women, the ancient face of Anna and the youthful face of Mary appear to merge for a moment. Luke turns to present the incident as the old eyes of Anna might have viewed it, seeing her former self in Mary, if only another road in life had been travelled. There is a hint of Anna's long ago virginity surrendered to love, now placed beside a virginity mysteriously preserved in spite of, yet also because of, an even greater love. Again, by telling us of Anna's long years of loneliness Luke seems to point toward the loneliness of Mary, the solitariness she will forever bear because of the immeasurable privilege given to her. All these things are hinted at in the subtle juxtapositioning of these two women. If this scene had ever been the subject of an opera. Mary and Anna would surely have been given at this point an aria sung in duet. I suspect Luke intends them to stand side by side on the timeless stage of the human mind, portraying a subtle counterpoint of femininity.

Even now Luke is not content with emphasizing only these aspects of Anna's life. He drives home the fact of her being a widow. The harsh lonely word is linked with a seeming immensity of human time in the words "eighty-four years." We know so well and so sadly how even the deepest loves can fade into forgetfulness under the weight of such years. Is this again an artist's subtle way of pointing beyond the joy of Mary in this present moment to the future Mother of Sorrows — an older

Mary, widowed first by the death of the strong artisan who
stands beside her on this shining day of family celebration,
then widowed even more terribly by the crashing of hammer
and cruel spike, the rending of flesh partly her own, the hoarse
agony she will be totally unable to respond to. Thus does Luke
with his artistry remind us that our joys and sorrow, our pas-
sions and pain, are somehow all experienced simultaneously,
each by a mystery blended into the other in spite of the deceptive separation and merciful illusion of time past, time present,
time future.

Anna has exchanged one passion for another. She has flung
herself from the embrace of arms long become limp and dead
to the arms of a God who is impervious to age and time. Anna
has ensured that years cannot again rob her of a chosen passion. This love affair is beyond the grasp of the tyrant time.
Mary has never known the breath-robbing embrace of human
intercourse. She has had to do no such forsaking. She has been
enfolded in an embrace so gentle as to exist beyond both sense
and touch, yet so mighty as to kindle life spontaneously within
her womb. Anna, Luke tells us, "did not depart from the
temple." It has become for her the home she lost long ago. The
temple houses her marriage to an intangible yet vividly perceived love. Mary goes another way to a different and costly
love affair with God. She does not need this temple, huge and
majestic and shining though it be. She herself has become the
temple in which God dwells.

For this fleeting moment they meet. Two women look into
one another's eyes. In Mary's eyes Anna sees the fear of the
unknown in this moment, a world of experience not under-
stood, a shadow, the look of the hunted. In Anna age has a
quiet strength, born to some extent of resignation yet able to
support the panic and weakness of youth. Her age brings to
bear all its considerable resources. Here is wisdom, tenderness,
insight. It pierces the deceptive ordinariness of this moment.
Anna's eyes look beyond the country girl and see a queen, her
hands stretch out to the swaddled infant and feel their

wrinkled finger tips catch fire with the as yet unformed majesty of kingship.

It has been said of a Chekhov play that, if when the curtain rises there is a weapon hanging on the wall, it will be used as a weapon before the play is over. In other words, there is no baggage carried either in the script or in the staging. If something is there, it is there for a purpose.

The gospels are like Chekhov plays. Almost nothing is extraneous. All is spare, economic, finely drawn. Everything is placed where it is for a certain purpose. It is not fortuitous that after the searing experience on the mount of Transfiguration, the disciples (and we) are confronted with human agony (possibly epilepsy) asking to be healed. This juxtaposition points us to the rhythm of all life fluctuating between mountain-top experience to valley experience, from celebration to duty, from ecstasy to responsibility. It is not by chance that on more than one occasion in the gospels, we read of a very ordinary person being healed of blindness, only to learn soon after of someone who suffers from incurable spiritual blindness. All these things serve a purpose in that long ago deceptively simple genre we call "gospel." The sequence is so well put together we are allowed the illusion sometimes that it is a series of simple stories — which paradoxically it also is — so simple that it can in large measure be told to a child.

Why then does Luke decide to include Simeon and Anna? I suspect that it is to make a link with all the long generations of prophecy. For so long there has been the certain hope, resilient and valiant in the face of countless crushing disappointments, that some day the representative of God would come into the temple and usher in a new age. The voices of that unconquerable expectation were mostly men, but Israel had also heard that hope expressed by its prophetesses. As Luke echoes those centuries of hope in the presence of Simeon, so he echoes the longing of generations of Hebrew women, one of whom would be the bearer of Messiah, in the presence of old Anna. Both in their seniority are symbols of the long years of expectation.

Prophecy has grown old. It needs the affirmation of the actual enfleshment of what it has hoped for.

Luke gives Simeon a song. We possess it as the hymn of evening, Nunc Dimittis, "Lord now lettest thou thy servant depart in peace." It is possible of course that, had we been in the temple among those who witnessed the incident, we would have heard the voice of Anna joining in that song. It is possible that Anna sang another song of the women of many generations when celebrating a birth. It was the wild ecstatic song of Hanna, when she had carried her newly born Samuel to the high and holy place at Shiloh, centuries before this joyful day. "My heart," sang that song, "exults in the Lord, my strength is exalted in the Lord. . . . I rejoice in thy salvation."

If she sang those ancient words, Anna would have sung her own Nunc Dimittis. She would ironically have sung the song that the young woman in front of her had sung while this child was still in her womb. "My soul," Mary sang, echoing Hanna, "doth magnify the Lord, and my spirit hath rejoiced in God my Saviour."

Like all great writers, Luke may also have given us levels of meaning that he himself was not aware of. As we approach the end of a century, we are aware that our world, particularly the western world, is growing older. Our population as a whole is becoming older, as fewer children are born and the aged live longer. For this reason Luke may have given our time a gift that will be increasingly significant for us as we come to this scripture for the rest of this century. Simeon and Anna emerge from the surrounding crowds that would have been coming and going in the temple at any time. It is significant that they are the ones who alone respond to the child's presence. Their dimming eyes are the eyes with a special vision. Their hands, withered and dry, are the hands that touch the child. Their voices are the voices that sing the song of the next day dawning.

It would seem as if Luke is giving to age a wisdom we find difficult to accord in western society. We do not turn to age as a source of vision. We presume that the vision of age is dim and entering the prison of physical limitation. Yet here in the temple it is otherwise. Age lifts up its voice and sings of hope. Age reaches out to touch the child in which it sees infinite possibility. Age sees a light. How can the light of Christ call contemporary old age to seek him in the present time? A great part of Christian pastoral ministry in the coming years will be to use all the revealed insights and skills of medicine, psychology, and sociology, to weave them into patterns of spirituality that can bring grace to the later years of life. We must become a community with such a temple that it will be possible for us all, in our Simeon and Anna years, to recognize the Child as he comes to us day by day.

Anna begins to speak, at first softly and reassuringly to the young couple, then to those standing around. Her voice begins to gather power as she speaks of their deepest expectations and hopes. Luke says that "she gave thanks to God, and spoke of him to all who were looking for the redemption of Jerusalem." Her rising voice belies her great age. It becomes something apart from her, of which she is instrument and channel. Those men and women around her, realizing themselves to be in the presence of aged yet ageless prophecy, bow their heads.

A Search for Healing

The people pressed round Jesus. And a woman who had had a flow of blood for twelve years and could not be healed by any one, came up behind him, and touched the fringe of his garment; and immediately her flow of blood ceased. And Jesus said, "Who was it that touched me?" When all denied it, Peter said, "Master, the multitudes surround you and press upon you!" But Jesus said, "Some one touched me; for I perceive that power has gone forth from me." And when the woman saw that she was not hidden, she came trembling, and falling down before him declared in the presence of all the people why she had touched him, and how she had been immediately healed. And he said to her, "Daughter, your faith has made you well; go in peace." Luke 8:42–48

• • •

We are all adept in the use of euphemism. Sometimes it is because we cannot bring ourselves to name something, it may be out of fear or guilt. There are times when euphemism is a device to mute the unavoidable terrors of human existence. Witness the inexhaustable ways in which we speak of death other than with that stark short syllable.

By such a device, in a mingled fear and well-intentioned tenderness, we speak of certain illnesses as a "condition." Very often what we mean is that someone must bear something from which there would seem to be no escape. It may be slight, or it may be utterly debilitating. Life can have become misery. Relationships, or the possibility of them, may have been destroyed. There may have been no physical agony, no points of crisis, no obvious disfigurements, but slowly and inexorably life may have become more confined, until it has ceased to be life and become mere existence.

Among the faces milling around Jesus, is such a person, a

woman. In that crowd she is only another face, yet for her, all of time is focused on this moment. Every faculty is concentrated on a purpose rapidly forming; every nerve is tremblingly alert. Hope and hopelessness are wrestling in her. She has become almost afraid to hope. Once she lived on it, now reluctantly it has become almost an enemy. Luke puts the reason for her wariness in two simple and terrible words: "twelve years." For twelve years the haemorrhage has flowed. Consider the average length of life in that day. Within that measure of time consider the few fleeting years of activity, well being, fulfillment. Half of that average adult stage of life has been drained away by an implacable enemy.

It may well have begun in the coming of potential new life to her youthful changing body, transforming her very fruitfulness into an emotional wilderness of fear and increasing resentment. She may well have seen all possibility of physical love die in that wilderness. Gradually the struggle would pass into a loneliness that would become in itself a pain greater and more corrosive than the physical discomfort. In the daily struggle to retain some vestige of physical attractiveness, to keep her body from becoming repulsive to those near her, all energy would eventually be consumed. Coupled with this would come the increasing tiredness that would make every action an effort of will.

Luke points to something else easily forgotten. "She could not," he says, "be healed by anyone." In these simple words he hints at the early struggle, the long ago conviction that the condition would pass, that life would come to her fully and beautifully, as it was coming to her friends. In time the hope would be disappointed, but with news of another possibility it would reassert itself. She would at first receive encouragement from a new physician; then would come mutual embarrassment and disappointment at his failure, and finally a thinly veiled mutual exasperation. Little by little self-esteem, self-worth, and trust are ended by this process. One cannot make the approach anymore. One retreats into defeat.

In her case there has now appeared one more possibility. She has heard of this man from Galilee who seems to have a healing gift. Even now it is not easy to respond to such a possibility directly, because the very hope can itself become the door to further bitterness. It is significant that at no time does she give any indication of wanting to make a direct approach to Jesus. In such a small rural world it would have been very possible to confront him as he approached or departed from the area. Another woman near the coast had done precisely this, as we know from the gospel story. But she approaches Jesus from behind. Why does Luke mention such a seemingly trivial thing, unless he does not regard it as trivial? Is it that approaching from behind somehow needs a lesser commitment to hope, and is therefore a defence against possible disappointment? Again, the indirect approach does not demand that she risk herself to any relationship. If you approach from behind, you do not have to face any eyes, particularly the eyes of any group or community. You do not have to reveal your desperation. You can remain anonymous. You make it possible to preserve that anonymity which year by year you have assumed — in which you want to hide, yet from which you also long desperately to escape.

She wishes, Luke tells us, only to touch the hem of Jesus' garment. There was a time she wished to tell about her condition, to be asked questions that might assist in its healing, to discuss ways of coping. All that is over. Now she takes refuge in the possibility of a "magical" touch.

Many people like this woman meet us today in the millions who sit watching religious television programs, seeking the longed for source of grace. Like her their approach to Christ is through a vast and anonymous crowd. Paradoxically the circumstance of television watching gives the illusion of complete self-centered individuality. In the electronic encounter no real relationship is offered or demanded. The person in the crowd retains, too, the ultimate defence of the off-on dial. Should the source of grace fail to satisfy, they have the power to eliminate.

Each person can shatter their own idol if it should prove ineffective in fulfilling their desires. Like the woman of Jesus' day they do not have to face the eyes of any community while having the illusion of nearness to grace. Finally, like her they can so easily arrive at a point when relationship is no longer wished for on the spiritual journey. All that is reached for is magic. The invitation to touch the television to find healing is at one and the same time a tribute to the timeless therapeutic power of touch and a parody of the reality.

As we watch her approach, knowing, or at least surmising, all that has gone before this moment, we realize again the magnificent resilience of human hope. It is something we see again and again to the almost indestructible. Even when under terrible suffering or sorrow it seems to die, hope needs only an encounter with some source of nourishment, some act of love, some gesture of tenderness, some word of encouragement, for it to flicker again into life. This is precisely why we can be so easily manipulated and victimized. In this instance an agonized woman, living in what has become almost a tomb, has perceived or heard in Jesus something that has penetrated the terrible layers of disappointment in her experience.

The logic of this for all of us leads to an almost paralyzing insight: there will come a day in our lives when we become to someone else what our Lord was to that woman on that occasion. Someday, quite surely, someone in great need will look to us as their source of help. We may find this very difficult to believe. We may not see ourselves as a potential help and strength to anybody at any time! The moment we think in such terms we are only too clearly aware of our own weaknesses and fears. But the need of another has for the moment transformed us from being ourselves in need to being a resource. We must respond. This realization in turn — that we must respond — can itself create a paralyzing fear of doing or saying the wrong thing. There is of course this possibility. A golden rule is to realize that the simpler the response, the more chance it has of being a helpful one. Many a time a person, turned to by another in some agony, has found themselves speechless in the face of the situation yet, by reaching out and touching, has allowed grace to flow into the need. We can be so paralysed by the wish to say the "right" thing or to do the "professional" thing, so anxious to use the "correct" technique, that we forget we have been placed there by God at that moment to be a channel of his love to another human being. The very realization of why we are there will in itself be a guide and resource to us, and will enable us to be a resource to the other person.

Sometimes our dread of becoming involved in someone else's life has about it a peculiar irony. We often cringe from being looked to for help. We may feel that the help requested is far beyond our capacity to give. Very often we realize how much, if not more, we ourselves need what the other seeks! Friends are at their wits end about their marriage. They turn to us, even though we may not be sure about our own. Friends turn to us because they need assurance in something they wrestle with, and we find we face the same doubts and the same fears. Friends turn to us in their dying and want to talk, and because of fear of our own death we cannot respond.

Perhaps we have only to realize something universal to make it easier for us to respond. It is simply that we turn toward one another far more often for understanding and companionship than for solutions. Often the reason we are turned to is not that we are thought to be different and strong and full of solutions, but precisely because we are known (far more than we may suspect!) to be ordinary and vulnerable and fallible, and therefore, for those reasons rather than because we are in any way superior, we will understand and respond.

It is useless to try to probe the mystery of the healing moment. Suffice it to say that it is instantaneous and total. No passionless diagnostic report could be crisper than the words of the evangelist: "Her flow of blood ceased." Because we read of her being healed, does not the analogy to television religious therapy break down? Two responses are in order. The first is that in her case she is healed by the reality of Christ present in flesh before her. She is in the presence, not of illusion, but of reality. The second is what happens after she realizes that she is physically healed.

The moment of contact is over. She has for so long surrounded herself with a protective solitude that her first instinct is to melt back into the crowd. So often we can be healed physically while psychically and socially remaining cripples. But she is not allowed to remain anonymous. The energizing mystery whom she has touched reaches out for her. Jesus says, "Who was it that touched me?" Peter's exasperation is understandable. There are too many faces, too many needs, too many demands. Peter expresses the strain and frustration of all contemporary helping professions. There are too many in the afternoon surgery, too many on the social worker's case load, too many couples in the marriage counsellor's offices. There are too many for the faces to focus, to become vivid individual human beings, each one complex and unique.

But not so with the person who now asks for this woman. This is he who has spoken of sparrows being sold for a farthing, yet not without the Creator of their seeming insignificance being aware of it. Now, as he stands surrounded by the crowd, he searches for a particular human being. By implication our Lord seems to be saying that even physical healing is not enough. Without the establishment of a relationship between healer and healed there is an incompleteness. Modern medical practice is frequently wary of personal involvement. Admittedly there can develop a demanding relationship, which asks more than can be given in professional circumstances. On the other hand there is sometimes discernible in medical practice a wish to substitute mere function and efficient application of procedures for relationship. This moment in the ministry of our Lord seems to suggest that healing and relationship are intimately linked.

What is now shown us is that loveliest of sights, the flowering of a human being. A face opens into beauty, a prisoner emerges from a cell, endless images come to the mind to celebrate it. Luke's words are richly suggestive: "When the woman saw that she was not hidden, she came trembling." No longer is there any reason for her to hide. She can emerge. She has gained freedom. She needs nothing to hide in, no shell of self-disgust, no protective armour of an assumed hopelessness, no denial of her own self-worth. She came trembling, but it is the trembling of suppressed energy, of new found vitality, a flow no longer draining but energizing.

Luke tells us that she "declared in the presence of all the people why she had touched him, and how she had been immediately healed." She who came from behind him to avoid human contact now is able to face a sea of eyes. She is able to take her place among others. The moment she begins to tell her story, all know that she has been healed. They do not necessarily know that blood has stopped flowing. They do not need to. They know that before them stands a human being who is vibrant with a new sense of wholeness. It seems as if our Lord forces her into the open for a purpose. I suspect Jesus seeks her socialization, which he sees as necessary to her complete healing as a person. The alienation of cell to cell has been overcome by his healing. Wholeness has been given to that complex commonwealth of the human body. Now it remains only that she, a cell long isolated from the body of the community, be restored and must begin the process of restoring herself.

As Luke brings his telling of this incident to an end, he uses a most significant word. He tells us that our Lord, addressing her, calls her "daughter." I cannot help but think it significant that when we first encounter her in the story, she is merely "a woman." The fact that before we part company she has become daughter, is a sign that, for her, relationship and love have again become possible.

A Drink of Water

Jesus had to pass through Sama'ria. So he came to a city of Sama'ria, called Sy'char, near the field that Jacob gave to his son Joseph. Jacob's well was there, and so Jesus, wearied as he was with his journey, sat down beside the well. It was about the sixth hour. There came a woman of Sama'ria to draw water. Jesus said to her, "Give me a drink." For his disciples had gone away into the city to buy food. The Samaritan woman said to him, "How is it that you, a Jew, ask a drink of me, a woman of Sama'ria?" For Jews have no dealings with Samaritans. Jesus answered her, "If you knew the gift of God, and who it is that is saying to you, 'Give me a drink,' you would have asked him, and he would have given you living water." The woman said to him, "Sir, you have nothing to draw with, and the well is deep; where do you get that living water? Are you greater than our father Jacob, who gave us the well, and drank from it himself, and his sons, and his cattle?" Jesus said to her, "Every one who drinks of this water will thirst again, but whoever drinks of the water that I shall give him will never thirst; the water that I shall give him will become in him a spring of water welling up to eternal life." The woman said to him, "Sir, give me this water, that I may not thirst, nor come here to draw." John 4:4–15

• • •

Over the millenia the ground level has changed. Nowadays you go down steps to the old well. You enter a gate in a high wall next to a busy strategically placed fruit stand; you walk through a pleasant garden to the roofless and never-completed shell of a Russian Orthodox church built around the well. There are two small sheds that house two flights of steep steps, one for going down, the other for returning. There is always a quiet priest on duty. A coin dropped into the well eventually splashes far below. The silence of its falling allows you to travel back across the long centuries to when a "wandering Aramean" named Jacob came here with his flocks. As to him so long ago, so to you, the water comes up cold and crystal clear.

You are standing in the heart of Samaria. In his gospel John says that Jesus "had to pass through Samaria." There is a hint that it was not readily chosen as a route. For generations Samaria had been, if not enemy territory, at least unfriendly. Jewish travellers did use the road, but carefully. There were bitter historical memories. Enmity had in time become hardened by religious prejudice. This is a viscious mingling, whether in ancient Samaria or modern Teheran, in Belfast or on the border country of India and Pakistan. There is too, for all of us, a Samaria we do not feel at ease passing through. There are territories in the interior of our lives where the past is painful. And in the exterior of our lives there are people we do not wish to encounter, areas of a city about which we have formed inherited prejudices or made ill informed stereotypes.

Jesus has gone through Samaria. It is about noon when he comes to this spot. Walking up the long gradient of the valley had drained him. He suggested to the others that they look for some food in the nearby village. He would stay for a while, try to find some shelter, if possible doze. John says that "Jesus, wearied as he was with his journey, sat down beside the well." We can treasure these moments of utter humanity in our Lord. They remove all elements of the unreality with which an anxious faith sometimes rushes to surround him. When we are capable of placing beside a stained glass window of Christ reigning in glory another window showing Jesus spreadeagled and slackjawed in the sleep of utter exhaustion, we will have taken a giant step toward affirming fully the mystery of Incarnation!

She may have come walking out of the blazing noonday sun, her shadow moving across him, making him open his eyes and stir. He may have wondered why she had come here, what urge for solitude or what social banishment brought her alone

to the well as a woman. Did he scent a human story behind her
solitary shadow across him? He felt parched lips and said simply, "Give me a drink." We do not think of our Lord as saying
"give me" to our humanity. That is what we instinctively say to
him as Lord. We say it in endless petition, allowable only by
our assurance of his endless love. But now, to this woman,
Jesus expresses the basic human need of a drink.

She is surprised at his speaking to her. She fences. She says
"How is it you, a Jew, ask a drink of me, a woman of Samaria?"
There may be here an element of sexual fencing. She presumes
that in the eyes of this Jewish man she as a Samaritan is to some
extent dehumanized, a female object. She realizes that sexual
invitations can begin deviously. It may be true that Jews do not
have dealings with Samaritans, but many histories have seen
such racial taboos crumble under the power of sexuality,
whether in South Africa or in the American Deep South or in a
world-wide colonial past. In her fencing she does not merely
mention her race but her sex. It may have been the basis for a
later intuition of Jesus which strikes home.

Deftly, still using the image of water, Jesus shifts ground. He
says "If you knew . . . who it is that is saying to you, 'Give me a
drink', you would have asked him, and he would have given
you living water." There is a hint of a hidden identity she is not
aware of, an invitation to something more subtle. But she is
wary. She chooses to stay with the known. There is even a little sarcasm, a suggestion that he is trying to impress. Hence the
barb in the question, "Are you greater than our father Jacob,
who gave us this well?"

Jesus, allowing the barb to go unanswered, very gently hints
again of another "water," another level of thirst our humanity
feels, another element of a quest worth pursuing. It is a request
for our attention that Christ puts to us all at the wells we come
to daily. The "well" is our occupation, the place of our professional expertise. The well is the office or the plant or the store
or the institution where we carry out our assigned role. The
Christ who encounters us asks that we consider an inner and

deeper meaning to what we do. Like this woman, when we are at these wells, we are often wary of being drawn into dialogue that smacks of the religious. We pride ourselves on being practical where it may be our only defense against something more powerful and therefore feared.

In the conversation that John reports in his gospel, the woman's armour of assumed practicality is pierced. The haunting image used by Jesus, "a spring of water welling up to eternal life," has resonated deep within her. She says, wonderingly and longingly, "Sir, give me this water . . ."

There are moments in us all when we confess to a longing we can scarcely admit to having. Most of us can do so only in moments of great intimacy or vulnerability. When we do, we are enriched beyond calculation. Sometimes such an admission of longing opens the way to taking out of our lives a great deal of internal garbage. If space is to be made for what is worth while, then what is not must be taken away. Quickly, like a surgeon who incises swiftly and deeply to extract a tumor, Jesus pierces to the very heart of what we euphemistically call her "life-style." "You have had five husbands, and he whom you now have is not your husband."

She panics for a moment and then rallies. "Sir, I perceive that you are a prophet." There is an effort at defensive irony. Then she diverts the threat of confronting her situation by a swift detour into religion. She points to the slope of Mount Gerazim looming over them. "Our fathers worshipped on this mountain; and you say that in Jerusalem is the place where men ought to worship."

It is a detour into religion, not into spirituality. The two can be quite different, the former often being mistaken for the latter, very often to the great impoverishment of a human life. Jesus counters almost brutally. He sweeps aside the pathetic attempt at diversion. "True worshippers," he says, "will worship the Father in spirit and in truth." Place is no longer to be relevant. The quality and reality of worship is to be the sole criteria. Just as there is a living water beyond physical water, so there is a spirituality beyond religion, a wisdom beyond mere information. This statement of our Lord has a ring of the kingdom about it. It is a counsel of perfection rather than a statement of things as they are or even will be. It is on a par with the great statements that open the Sermon on the Mount. It is an absolute that calls us to reach out to its fulfillment.

It may well be that a time will come when the worship of men and women will be totally spiritual, but that time is not yet. Worship is still defined by denomination and tradition. It is still, with most of us, deeply committed to a certain place, be it meeting room or chapel or cathedral. We resonate to a particular kind of language. As witness to this is the fact that most conflicts in Christian communities are about either of these two things, space or language. Attempts to change either usually meet with at best rigorous questioning and at worst outright refusal. No wonder the woman seized on the issue of where worship should more properly be done, on nearby Mount Gerazim in Samaria or on Mount Zion in Jerusalem. She had heard the endless arguments going on around her for as long as she could remember. What better way to escape from the probing conversation of this Jewish traveller. But the traveller will not allow her to escape by this route. He rigourously blocks the turning of their conversation to the irrelevant. There is something more important than discussing the "where" of worship.

In today's church it is obvious that our Lord is demanding that Christian life see these issues for what they really are — secondary. Our Lord does not regard them as irrelevant. As long as we are human, we will have certain spatial needs. We will respond or react to design, colour, architecture. The tradition we are part of will be richer or poorer according to how the physical space for its expression serves the purpose. The praise we offer and the intercession we lift will be the richer or poorer according to the quality of language we decide to use for their expression. All such things have their validity. However, these things are not in themselves ends but rather means.

The life of any Christian community will be judged not on the functional perfection of its sanctity for worship nor on the felicity of language, however majestic or lyrical it be. This is ultimately what our Lord is saying to us today, through that single stern sentence to the woman who faced him at Jacob's well.

She makes one last effort to blunt the piercing of her armour. Her's is the armour we all don against the confrontation with ultimate things. "I know that Messiah is coming," she says. It is a very human ploy. The present threat is deflected by placing the issue in the future. We are so easily and so often "too busy at the moment" to deal with spiritual things. There will be, we maintain, a more suitable time and place. It is always an indefinable time and an unspecified place. The good reason for this is that neither time nor place are intended to be given reality. But as with Jesus and the woman in this encounter, so with Christ and each one of us. His presence is in the present moment. His question demands a response now. The name of him who encounters at the well of our unacknowledged thirst is not "I will be some day." His name is I AM.

A Man Under Authority

Now a centurion had a slave who was dear to him, who was sick and at the point of death. When he heard of Jesus, he sent to him elders of the Jews, asking him to come and heal his slave. And when they came to Jesus, they besought him earnestly, saying, "He is worthy to have you do this for him, for he loves our nation, and he built us our synagogue." And Jesus went with them. When he was not far from the house, the centurion sent friends to him, saying to him, "Lord, do not trouble yourself, for I am not worthy to have you come under my roof; therefore I did not presume to come to you. But say the word, and let my servant be healed. For I am a man set under authority, with soldiers under me: and I say to one, 'Go,' and he goes; and to another, 'Come,' and he comes; and to my slave, 'Do this,' and he does it. When Jesus heard this he marveled at him, and turned and said to the multitude that followed him, "I tell you, not even in Israel have I found such faith." And when those who had been sent returned to the house, they found the slave well. Luke 7:2-10

•   •   •

A line of trees shelters the ruins of Capernaum from the wind that sweeps from the west across the north end of the lake. They are extensive ruins, and digging is steadily going on year by year. One building alone stands above the small house foundations that pit the ground southward toward the water. Built in the third century, it is a reconstruction of an even older synagogue that stood on this site. Great stones lie around. The four pillars still standing support the ancient roofends. If one looks carefully, one notices many symbols carved into the stone. Strangely, because this building has always been a synagogue, there are not only Jewish symbols, which one would expect, but there are also Roman symbols. Two in particular are interesting. Two eagles carved back to back remain to tell us that this place had some connection with the Tenth Legion. The other symbol is a laurel wreath within which is a seashell. This was the decoration given to a Roman soldier who has saved the life of an officer in battle.

Why are such things carved into this ancient synagogue? Even though the Romans were the occupying power here, one would have thought the last thing to be incorporated into these stones would be Roman insignia. Was there a link between this community and the garrison that once kept the local Pax Romana in this provincial fishing town?

Let time change this place for us. We are standing in the Capernaum of Jesus' day. The town is of course anything but quiet and deserted. It is the bustling hub of the north end of the lake. We can see the synagogue standing above the small houses. It is similar to one that will eventually replace it and will last into the far away twentieth century. If we were to stand on the quayside on a Sabbath, we might want to visit the synagogue. As Gentiles we would sit at the back. We could see and hear what was going on. Quite probably, in that special section, we would notice a figure whose civilian clothes fail to disguise the rugged face and toughened body of a Roman centurion.

They have a name for him here in the synagogue, for him and for the other Gentiles who from time to time drop in during worship time. They call them "God-fearers." They are thoughtful searching men and women who seek meaning and hope in an empire whose many gods have never quieted the hunger of humanity. The late twentieth century is peopled with such, longing for a community to be part of, for a faith to be a resource for their lives — a light of hope in the sometimes hopeless wilderness of today's world.

Such people often stand in well dressed agnosticism at a friend's funeral, or sing lustily and nostalgically the carols of Christmas. They accept, with a little guilt and much appreciation, the invitation to be godparent on the basis of trusted friendship. They feel, and sometimes express, an undefined anger toward the church, being a little unsure whether to blame it for changing or for not changing. A former faith has died, yet the pain and complexity of the contemporary world creates a longing for a view of reality that will provide meaning and hope. Such are modern God-fearers. Now, as then, there sit among the God-fearers some magnificent human beings, repelled and yet haunted by God.

Look again at this man sitting in the shadows of the synagogue. Because of an incident not yet begun, he will be immortalized in the sacred writings of a tradition still to be created. By his direct manner, by his insight gained from seeing a great deal of life in various parts of the world, he will affect the thinking of a Jewish teacher in a way that will have incalculable consequences. Ironically he has no name. He appears in Luke's gospel: "A centurion had a slave dear to him, who was sick and at the point of death."

It is a measure of this man's concern that he decided to approach Jesus at all. The representatives of occupying powers seldom impress either the people they rule or their own superiors by showing dependence. This may well be a factor in his decision to approach Jesus indirectly. "He sent to him elders of the Jews, asking him to come and heal his slave." He may well have been guarding his flank against future criticism should there be a refusal from the rabbi, or should the rabbi fail. All of us extend our trust or risk ourselves as carefully as possible. We are all conscious of the glass-house through which the world looks at us. We will not do this or that because of what others may think. We cannot go to this or that place because of our position in the community. We possess, and are possessed by, image and role and status. We are all under a thousand trivial and frequently self-imposed authorities, real or imagined. We serve them with consistent loyalty, often at the cost of our deepest needs and longings.

Those whom he sent to Jesus pressed his case without reserve. "He is worthy to have you do this for him," they said, "for he loves our nation, and he built us our synagogue." No wonder they were so insistent! He stands forever as the proto-type of a phenomenon known in every Christian congrega-tion, the donor who is not quite sure that he or she wishes to be involved in the life of the community they generously support with special gifts. They have their own agenda, as we say, not necessarily to be shared with those they benefit. Yet often, behind the reserve and the detachment, there is a longing. There may be past loyalties, worn away by disappointment or hurt or cynicism, but enduring at some level.

When Matthew in his gospel recalls this incident, he tells us that the centurion actually came to Jesus himself. It is not necessarily a contradiction of Luke's version. It is very possible that both events could have taken place. Jesus may have hesi-tated. He may have suspected some social or political trap to discredit him. He may have been the prisoner of a natural Jewish exclusiveness about his ministry to this point. It is not the only time this shows in him. It may have been necessary for the Roman to come out himself to Jesus, and to take the risk of public rejection by the rabbi. If that was the case, it is further tribute to the depth of his concern for the sick servant in his house.

Human nature is complex. Here is a man obviously reflec-tive about life and its meaning, obviously admired, even by those for whom he represents a foreign domination. Yet listen to his self assessment when he attempts to intercept Jesus as he comes toward the house. "When he was not far from the house, the centurion sent friends to him, saying to him, 'Lord, do not trouble yourself, for I am not worthy to have you come under my roof; therefore I did not presume to come to you'." There is an attractive quality about this admission. It hints of something very human. How frequently we find that the very person highly thought of by others had a very low sense of self-esteem!

But there is one thing this decent man was quite clear about. Everything in his training and make-up had helped him to recognize it. He knew natural authority when he met it. This he made perfectly clear in his magnificent assessment of Jesus. "Say the word," he suggests to Jesus, "and let my servant be healed. For I am a man set under authority, with soldiers under me: and I say to one, 'Go,' and he goes; and to another, 'Come', and he comes; and to my slave, 'Do this', and he does it."

We live at a time when authority is instinctively denied a high place in our vocabulary. Our very individualistic culture makes us wary of authoritive claims over us. We are cynical of social and political authorites, questioning of intellectual ones. Spiritually we place a high value on our own subjective experience. Yet over the centuries Christianity has learned that there is such a thing as spiritual authority. There are souls to whom we should accord an authority in spiritual matters. They will not always be our superior, nor seem to be even our equal by other-worldly standards. But spiritually they go before us and stand on the God-ward side of us.

Of Christ himself we so easily, in a democratic age, forget that we entitle him as our Lord. We have got so used to it that we can miss its deep challenge to contemporary instincts and attitudes. It claims authority by its very nature as a title. The language of the two words *our Lord* sounds above contemporary language. Other concepts of Jesus the Christ suggest intimacy, friendship, companion, guide, lover. Many of these concepts of our Lord have a legitimacy that does not prevent them from lending themselves at worst to sentimentality. The concept of *our Lord* brings to our relationship with him elements of obedience, loyalty, service, discipline, without which faith can be nothing more than a contemptible and self-serving dependency.

The centurion's statement brought an instant response from Jesus. (Matthew gives the fuller account, but Luke describes only the beginning of it.) Luke hears Jesus say, "I tell you, not even in Israel have I found such faith." Not only does Jesus say that, but Luke tells us that he turned and spoke to the multitude that followed him. On the whole, this is out of character for Jesus and is a measure of the effect the incident had on him. If he had any feelings that he was sent "only to the lost sheep of the house of Israel" (to quote him on another occasion), those feelings were deeply challenged at this moment. They were challenged by this simple Roman soldier's recognition of the profound moral authority he felt himself to be encountering in this Jewish rabbi.

Years later the recalling of this incident was to have a profound effect on the outreach of the early Christian communities. Formed at first mainly of Jews, they would look back to the moment when centurion and rabbi met in the narrow Capernaum street. There would be those who would see the exclamation of Jesus as pointing to a world-wide rather than a merely Jewish mission. Incidents such as this would launch the great "Gentile mission" of Paul. Ironically, by his compliment to the rabbi from nearby Nazareth, an unknown Roman soldier provided the impetus for a new faith eventually to reach Rome itself, to capture its heart, and to journey far beyond. So is the course of history changed, not necessarily by the decisions of the great, but by unnumbered daily incidents, when the unknown and the seemingly unimportant are the instruments by whom God builds the world.

An Uninvited Guest

*Behold, a woman of the city, who was a sinner, when she
learned that he was at table in the Pharisee's house, brought an
alabaster flask of ointment, and standing behind him at his
feet, weeping, she began to wet his feet with her tears, and
wiped them with the hair of her head, and kissed his feet, and
anointed them with the ointment. Now when the Pharisee who
had invited him saw it, he said to himself, "If this man were a
prophet, he would have known who and what sort of woman
this is who is touching him, for she is a sinner." And Jesus
answering said to him, "Simon, I have something to say to
you." And he answered, "What is it, Teacher?" "A certain
creditor had two debtors; one owed five hundred denarii, and
the other fifty. When they could not pay, he forgave them
both. Now which of them will love him more?" Simon
answered, "The one, I suppose, to whom he forgave more."
And he said to him, "You have judged rightly." Then turning
toward the woman he said to Simon, "Do you see this woman?
I entered your house, you gave me no water for my feet, but
she has wet my feet with her tears and wiped them with her
hair. You gave me no kiss, but from the time I came in she has
not ceased to kiss my feet. You did not anoint my head with
oil, but she has anointed my feet with ointment. Therefore I
tell you, her sins, which are many, are forgiven, for she loved
much; but he who is forgiven little, loves little." And he said to
her, "Your sins are forgiven."* Luke 7:37–48

• • •

She haunts the memory of the gospel writers. Every one of
them recalls the sudden vivid moment when she came into
their lives, did what she had to do, then disappeared again.
Although some of the tradition longs to identify her with Mary
of Magdala, there is no evidence for this. She comes quite liter-

ally out of the shadows and returns to them without a name. But for the short while she is on the stage of the gospel, she is the absolute focus of attention. Her action assumed that.

Luke says simply that she "was a sinner." The word *Sinner* must have had a specific connotation, as it is not in character for Luke to be judgemental. He may, however, be voicing the timeless contempt of society for the prostitute. Later in the evening, perhaps just a few moments after the episode, Simon, the host, remarked in sarcastic surprise that Jesus did not know "who and what sort of a woman" the intruder was. Again the implication would seem to be prostitution.

As suddenly as she came she is gone. One can almost imagine those who saw her wondering afterward whether her visit had actually happened or whether she were something dreamt, a half remembered figure from the muddled images of a long convivial evening. All four evangelists speak of that evening when Jesus was invited to a meal. In three of the tellings there are certain consistencies. All three place the meal in the home of a Pharisee. Two name the host as Simon. But the single constant element in all four evangelists is the woman and what she did. Whoever she was, she had a superb instinct for what would communicate her otherwise inexpressible feelings.

Luke's language in Greek lets us know that it was no casual drop-in occasion. The meal that night was a very formal one. This point is significant for understanding what happened. In the house of a socially prominent man, particularly of the party called the Pharisees, only a formal meal would be taken in the Graeco-Roman manner. The guests would recline on couches. This would make the feet of the guests, especially when bared of their sandals as they would be, available to the touch of anyone coming from behind.

It is also just possible that an invitation to Jesus on an occasion of such formality was a form of social intimidation. Socially it was a long way from the local customs of a Galilean village to a dinner party that aped the formalities of the Empire. There may have been a wish on Simon's part to issue an invitation to this subversive if intriguing rabbi, lay out the most elaborate table, invite some sophisticated friends, act out the latest etiquette and conversation from Antioch or Rome, and show this Nazarene his place by obvious social humiliation. It would not be the first or last time the method would be used. When Mahatma Ghandi was building his following in the villages of India, senior British Army officers and diplomats attempted on more than one occasion the very same device, with exactly the same success as Simon experienced at his expensive table twenty centuries before. As for most of us, we have been guilty of at least the casual disparaging remark after a guest has left our table.

In Jesus' day the formal banquet often gathered around its edges the curious and the less fortunate. They stood in the archways or colonnade around the banquet room of a large villa. To a certain point this was accepted and allowed. So someone who desperately wished to communicate with Jesus could easily approach.

She comes in, staying in the shadows outside the table lights. The guests are lying on their couches supported on one elbow in the empire's fashion. She crouches down so that her approach goes unnoticed for some time. Her subsequent actions reveal a human being for whom words have become quite inadequate. There is too much emotion. It may have been gratitude for a kindness, for some deep and indescribably personal wholeness discovered through contact with this man. This we do not know. But we do know that the power of what is waiting to be expressed can be released only in action. In the very deepest meaning of the phrase, she cannot merely speak love, she must somehow make love.

The first release is tears. For her to speak to Jesus, in his position on the couch, she would have had to confront all eyes. She touches him at the nearest available point of his body. Tears, hot and wet, fall on his feet, her hands sweeping them away as soon as they fall, her long black hair envelopes his limbs as her head sways back and forth in the intensity of her outburst. By now she is noticed. All eyes move from the woman to Jesus as the recipient of her attentions. He has every right literally to kick her away from him. She is a woman of little or no reputation. She is uninvited. Around the table, among those who know her unsavoury reputation in the community, her actions arouse a mocking amusement. A long necked jar appears in her hands, a heavy scented expensive oil cascades over Jesus' ankles and feet. Her hands tenderly and expressively flow as she bathes him in her gift. The murmuring begins.

Jesus is aware of what is being thought if not fully said. As on many such occasions, the remarks are probably made quite audibly in the presence of the woman but in a way that indicates her presence is totally irrelevant. The woman is totally dehumanized, reduced to an object.

The eyes of Simon and Jesus lock. Guest and host have no illusions about one another. Jesus perceives the contempt this whole occasion is designed to express, under the guise of hospitality. The dinner has been for one purpose, to size up this popular peasant, to assess the significance of his popularity and his quality as a human being. For Simon the mere suggestion of a link between his guest and this unsavoury female is proof of what he has suspected. If this peasant had any sense of judgement about people, he would know the damage this kind of thing would do him in the eyes of decent people. As Luke tells it, "When the Pharisee who had invited him saw it, he said to himself, 'If this man were a prophet, he would have known who and what sort of woman this is who is touching him, for she is a sinner'."

Every thought of Simon is communicated in the eye to eye contact between him and his guest. Jesus does not flinch. He simply says, "Simon, I have something to say to you." The reply is smooth, the last word a whiplash of sarcasm. "What is it, Teacher?" says Simon.

There wells up in Jesus a rare moment of revulsion and rage, a resentment against the insensitivity and viciousness being perpetrated. It is of course fundamentally directed at himself, but it encompasses the woman. It uses her as the instrument to wound him; therefore it wounds her. She is a pawn, a convenient device by which to destroy him. Only he, if anyone, knows the reason and the possible cost of this action on her part. He is also aware how the love she has shown can so easily be sneered at in sleazy after-dinner witticisms.

Restraining his rage Jesus speaks at first with deliberate indirectness. In a simple and obvious parable he puts a question. Simon, still humoring this guest whom he hopes to embarrass, listens. Jesus uses the image of money, thus making shrewd assessment of the priorities of his fellow guests and of his host. He speaks of a forgiving creditor who receives immense gratitude from one who had owed and been forgiven an immense debt. Yes, his host, obviously bored if a little puzzled, understands the reference and answers Jesus' question.

Then with cold and deliberate precision Jesus enumerates the slight but effective ways by which, as host, Simon has communicated his contempt and patronage. There has been no welcoming water for washing, no receiving kiss of peace, no oil to scent the body of a welcome and honoured guest. The reason for the absence of all these, Jesus implies, is the absence on Simon's part of even minimal respect, not to mind affection. Around the table, hidden by the subtle niceties of social obligation, there exists an obscene and impenetrable lovelessness. The table lights illuminate hypocrisy and, at a deeper level, hatred. It is a hatred, as we know, that in a few months, will transform the guest into a prisoner. Only in the shadows beyond the table, only in this woman whom Jesus now looks at, has love been shown. Only in this woman, the one human being dismissed by everyone in the room, is there an ability to discern the exceptional quality and significance of what in Jesus has touched and transformed her. By her realization that she can pour out her deepest agony to him, she has gained the capacity to achieve an acceptance and wholeness that Simon and his sophisticated friends will never discover. She, Jesus says, has given all; they have given nothing. "He who is forgiven little," remarks Jesus, "loves little." She has poured herself out; they crouch in hardened shells of assumed self-sufficiency. She has opened herself to the entry of love; they have slammed innumerable doors against love's very possibility.

It is typical of Jesus that the woman is never lost sight of. She becomes the focus of his attention as he turns from his rebuke of Simon. She receives the ultimate affirmation. To her he says, "Your sins are forgiven." Around the table there are gasps of amazement at such presumption. The sarcasm is obvious in at least one voice overheard. "Who is this, who even forgives sins?" But the guest is no longer listening. For him there is only one person present who is capable of hearing what he has to say or of receiving what he has to give. To the woman Jesus says, "Your faith has saved you; go in peace."

This incident is at the centre of the Christian faith, and at the heart of the human situation. The terrible irony, in the protest against Jesus declaring sins forgiven, derives from the fact that every single human being must learn this mysterious power, this sacred obligation, to forgive sins. If we are to be mature, we must come to a point where we are capable of forgiving others, precisely because we accept the fact that God has forgiven us. It was to drive this central point home that Jesus would one day say to his disciples that their prayers had to be conditioned by this one issue alone. They could pray "forgive us our sins" so long as they realized that it is possible to receive such forgiveness only "as we forgive those who sin against us." It is not an arbitrarily imposed condition. It is simply the way in which life, spiritually and psychologically and in every other way, works. The source of forgiveness is divine, but the channel of forgiveness is our forgiving humanity.

A Liberated Woman

Early in the morning Jesus came again to the temple; all the people came to him, and he sat down and taught them. The scribes and the Pharisees brought a woman who had been caught in adultery, and placing her in the midst they said to him, "Teacher, this woman has been caught in the act of adultery. Now in the law Moses commanded us to stone such. What do you say about her?" This they said to test him, that they might have some charge to bring against him. Jesus bent down and wrote with his finger on the ground. And as they continued to ask him, he stood up and said to them, "Let him who is without sin among you be the first to throw a stone at her." And once more he bent down and wrote with his finger on the ground. But when they heard it, they went away, one by one, beginning with the eldest, and Jesus was left alone with the woman standing before him. Jesus looked up and said to her, "Woman, where are they? Has no one condemned you?" She said, "No one, Lord." And Jesus said, "Neither do I condemn you; go, and do not sin again." John 8:2–11

• • •

For centuries men and women, when they come to marriage, have used a word of immense beauty and deep meaning. It is the word *honour*. It's use may vary slightly as liturgy evolves, but it always carries the same great weight of meaning. We are asked if we are prepared "to love and to honour," or we will say, "I honour you in the name of God." At such a moment one is promising to honour the full humanity of the other person, to give him or her the honour of being a complete and separate being other than oneself. One is promising that one will never regard the other as mere object, as an extension of one's own desires or purposes or ambitions. In a sentence, to promise to honour someone is to promise not to use them.

In every relationship he entered into, from the most intimate to the most casual, our Lord honoured other people. At no time is anyone made a stepping stone to someone else. Nobody is cultivated because they may be useful to his purposes. Nobody is seen as an object. Times without number we are guilty of this. We possess endless justification for our lapses. People come to be seen as "useful" to our cause. Since our cause is impeccable, there is of course no harm in our using them! This man should be cultivated because he can gain us entry into strategic places; this woman, because she is a potential donor to our cause. Naturally, we are not using such a person, since what could be more for their good than to become involved in our good purposes? The line is a subtle one, and is easily and frequently crossed.

To use others for any reason — for their influence, their money, their power — is the essence of the wilderness experience we know in the gospel as the temptation of our Lord. Emerging from that experience he opts for the development of relationships that call out, for certain men and women, their deepest loyalty. In every case it is obvious that they are sought for no reason other than themselves. Not one of that original band he called about him are sought as a means to some other end. To every one of them Jesus gives full honour. Because of this quality in him, of honouring people, there comes for our Lord a moment that, underneath its outer studied calm, is one of rage, a depth of rage that could be dealt with only by silence.

The incident takes place in a very public area and at a very public moment. This was not accidental. We are at a stage in his ministry when Jesus had begun not only to catch the attention of political circles, but to become regarded as potential trouble. Also, he is in the temple, teaching and conversing with those who gather to hear him. It was a normal everyday sight in the great court yard. Jesus used it, but not frequently. We get the strong impression from the gospel that Jerusalem is not where he most wishes to be. In general, Galileans felt uncomfortable in the more formal and conservative world of the capital. We can safely assume that, on this occasion, Jesus is perfectly aware he is not wholly in the company of friends; somewhere in the group is an ear listening, so that his words can be reported, cold-bloodedly analysed, and, if possible, warped out of context and meaning.

It is now early morning. He is using the few hours before the sun will blaze down on the flagstones. He is probably expecting trouble. The previous day he has had to deal with no less than a platoon of temple police hovering about, waiting for some excuse to move in. Suddenly he sees a group approaching. As they move through the listeners, they prove to be very obviously significant public figures. With one exception all are men. In front of them, obviously torn between intense embarrassment and sheer terror, urged on roughly and unceremoniously, is a woman. The new arrivals halt. The gospel writer describes the scene vividly. He speaks of the men making her stand in full view of everybody.

The waiting silence is cut brutally and succinctly. A voice announces that she has been "caught in the act of adultery." The voice goes on to invoke the terrible traditional punishment (seldom applied): death by stoning. In two sentences sex and violence have been linked as neatly as in any screaming tabloid headline. The obscenity lies not in any sexual act but in the fact that there is not even a pretense that the incident has been contrived for any reason other than to compromise Jesus publicly. He must be confronted as openly as possible. If the issue can be based on a matter of sexuality, so much the better. The method and the content will become the stuff of political hachetry down the centuries.

It is a most dangerous moment for Jesus. Doubtless the temple police of yesterday are near although out of sight. He has to think clearly and quickly. His ability is probably not helped by the nausea he feels at the brutal use being made of the unfortunate woman. To our Lord at this moment we can be certain that she, as a human being, is paramount. What she may or may not have done, in comparison with her humanity is irrelevant. The real prostitution of the self is being committed by those who dragged her here. Jesus risks no eye to eye engagement. The situation is too volatile. Sitting on a step, as he may have been, he doodles in the dust of the flagstones, his mind racing. He continues to do this even when another voice, sensing his seeming retreat, demands a reply.

There can be a peculiar power to quietness and stillness under stress. Sometimes an attack can be blunted. The situation can even be brought under one's control. Jesus looks up and says a single electrifying sentence that engenders its own far longer stunned silence. "Let him who is without sin among you, be the first to throw a stone at her." It is a dare, a risk, a challenge. It confronts them on their own chosen ground of law. However, this is not a question of cerebral law but of inner conscience. It turns all eyes away from the victimized woman, who is seen as an object. It turns all those who hear it toward themselves, making each one look into his own self as object, unattractive though that may be.

Jesus says nothing more. The scene is frozen. He again drops his attention to the ground. He has pierced to the quick. In another sense he has paid the group a compliment. He has given each man the possibility of becoming his true self. He has stung each man into awareness of the obscenity of his act. Together they have made a human being into a thing, a political device. In terms of their own legalism they have shown themselves to be potential murderers. To rob someone of their essential being is to do violence to them, to dishonour them. In contemporary society we do this a great deal. We do this with the current movie or television queen or king, with the face and body of the voluptuous magazine fold-out, even with public political figures. Granted that in these cases the people themselves concur in the process, we are still guilty of reducing them to disposable objects. We dishonour their humanity.

In the silence that follows Jesus' statement, there comes to each a certain realization. One by one, feet stir and turn to go.

The original listeners, aware that there is political agenda, perhaps even physical danger, have already gone. Only the woman stays. It is intriguing that she does. It is possible of course that she is simply too terrified to stir. She could be totally drained of the will to make even a minor decision. I suspect she stayed for the reason that all of us would have stayed. We wish to stay where we have been affirmed and put back together again, where the shambles of our deepest selves have been made whole.

After a long time Jesus looks up. It is no more than a recognition of his full humanity to say that he may well have been waiting for his own fear and tension to subside. Incarnation includes adrenalin as one of its ingredients, surely! He asks, "Has no one condemned you?" He is perfectly aware of this being the case. It is almost as if he wishes her to state that liberating fact herself. She says, "No one, Lord." Jesus replies, "Neither do I condemn you; and do not sin again."

It is not a dismissal. It is a liberation. It recognizes her ability to make her own decision. Jesus honours her so that she will be enabled to honour herself, to know herself as the affirmed and liberated woman she really is. It is particularly significant that our Lord obviously honours her, while also obviously assuming that she actually did what she was originally charged with! His statement, "Go, and do not sin again," points precisely to this. Yet, in spite of this, there is no lessening of his affirmation of her as a human being.

We see here in Jesus two great gifts that are particularly valuable in human relationships of any kind. He possesses the ability to see the truth within a person, the truth we all sometimes try to hide but reveal in a score of subtle ways to the sensitive observer. John, in his gospel, says of Jesus that "he knew what was in men." The other gift we see here in our Lord is that of confronting somebody without alienating them, making it possible for another person to become accountable, even to receive criticism, while at the same time retaining their trust, even their affection. Later, this act, with other decisions and actions, will cost Jesus his life. In the meantime this incident in his ministry will open up, for countless men and women, a shining way to their own liberation if, in their living, they choose to take that Way toward others and toward themselves.

A further note may shed light on this poignant encounter. Although the story is usually found in John's gospel, as the opening verses of chapter 8, in some translations of the Bible it is found at the end of John's gospel. Many feel that it is actually a piece of Luke's gospel, and it has often been linked with Luke 21:38. I think that in character and tone and attitude the incident is totally in keeping with the instincts of that gentle and sensitive man.

The Risen One

The Lake

*After this Jesus revealed himself again to the disciples by the
Sea of Tibe'ri-as; and he revealed himself in this way. Simon
Peter, Thomas called the Twin, Nathan'a-el of Cana in Galilee,
the sons of Zeb'edee, and two others of his disciples were
together. Simon Peter said to them, "I am going fishing." They
said to him, "We will go with you." They went out and got into
the boat; but that night they caught nothing. Just as day was
breaking, Jesus stood on the beach; yet the disciples did not
know that it was Jesus. Jesus said to them, "Children, have you
any fish?" They answered him, "No." He said to them, "Cast the
net on the right side of the boat, and you will find some." So
they cast it, and now they were not able to haul it in, for the
quantity of fish. That disciple whom Jesus loved said to Peter,
"It is the Lord!" When Simon Peter heard that it was the Lord,
he put on his clothes, for he was stripped for work, and sprang
into the sea. But the other disciples came in the boat, dragging
the net full of fish, for they were not far from the land, but
about a hundred yards off. When they had finished breakfast,
Jesus said to Simon Peter, "Simon, son of John, do you love me
more than these?" He said to him, "Yes, Lord; you know that I
love you." He said to him, "Feed my lambs."* John 21:1-8, 15

• • •

Bereavement immobilizes. No other human experience can do
so with greater power. In the face of bereavement nothing
seems worth doing. There is a lassitude in the limbs, a passivity
of the mind. Sometimes the best intentioned actions or words
of friends are of no avail. Eventually, if life pursues its normal
healthy course, there comes a moment when the prison door
opens on traumatized emotions and paralysed thinking, and
we take a step. It may be a very small one. It may even be that

we are not conscious of taking it at the time but, looking back, we realize that, in a particular moment, we took the first step on the road back to life.

In such a moment, some weeks after he had experienced things so terrible and so mysterious that he was incapable of fully assimilating them, Simon Peter said simply and decisively, "I am going fishing."

To do what we are trained to do, what we have always done, is to say who we are. In some sense we are what we do. That is why, if we come to hate what we do, we can eventually come to hate ourselves. For Simon Peter fishing was a way of getting back his hold on a shattered universe. Many people have found sanity in the face of disintegrating sorrow by resuming the routine they know best. We move back to it as a secondary level of meaning, when the ultimate level of meaning for us, the relationship, has been broken.

The other disciples said to him, "We will go with you." Very often, our breaking out of the emotional prison of bereavement also frees others who are involved in our lives. A bereaved employer can place employees in a kind of prison where there is loss of direction, lack of planning, doubt about the future. An immobilized family member can put other family members in a prison where they are not able to make decisions, perhaps cannot even express their feelings. It may well have been an eager and relieved chorus of voices around Peter who said, "We will go with you."

It is typical of the honesty and realism of the Bible that John doesn't hesitate a moment in saying that it was a disastrous expedition. He sums up those interminable hours in five devastating words: "That night they caught nothing."

There is no guarantee that the first attempts at rebuilding a shattered reality will be successful. The sudden new resolve is not necessarily sufficient in itself. We may fail to think clearly. We may be impulsive, even manic. We can be so desperate to prove that life has begun again that the sudden burst exhausts itself and ends in a paroxysm of tears. This may be at a desk, in the kitchen, on a walk, in the car at a traffic light. But what is all important is that, however disastrously the first effort ends, it has at least begun. The morning of the next chapter of life has at least broken. The night of sorrow, at least in the sense of unbroken darkness, is over. John says of the disciples' experience, "As day was breaking, Jesus stood on the beach."

As with the disciples, so with us. When we are living in the early dawning of emotional recovery, we are still perceiving the world through a haze of residual effects of our agony — chiefly physical and emotional weariness. Even if we have a deep Christian faith, we do not necessarily realize that the figure encountered in our wilderness between bereavement and recovery is Christ our risen Lord. We see sometimes only a friend who has dropped in or who asks us for lunch. We hear only a voice on the phone, only the mail man with a letter, only a priest with a chalice of wine. It is still the daybreak of emotional recovery, and everything is half hidden in a mist of conflicting feelings. And so there is a universal reality within that long ago lakeside moment. John says, "The disciples did not know that it was Jesus."

The figure on the shore asks a question that does not seem particularly helpful. "Have you any fish?" Yet, by asking them about their fishing, he allows them to declare (very bluntly!) their sense of frustration and failure. For the most part we are usually afraid to help someone express this, indeed, we are usually afraid to admit even to ourselves.

Having asked the question and received their obviously disgruntled reply, the risen Lord suggests what we sometimes hesitate to suggest, because it seems so mundane. We who feel compelled always to have a new idea or the latest therapy technique, hesitate to say quietly what sounded across that quiet morning lake. In effect Christ said, "Try again." "Cast the net on the right side of the boat and you will find some." Notice the powerful suggestion in "You will find some." There is power in the quiet simple suggestion that we act with the expectation that something will be achieved.

When fish are found, there is a sudden realization that a familiar pattern is being played out. But what is interesting is the response we see. John, with quick discernment, shouts, "It is the Lord"! Peter springs into the water. The others come to shore "dragging the net full of fish." We see three spiritual gifts vividly portrayed in these varied responses. In John's response we see the gift of insight — intuitive, sometimes even ecstatic. In Peter we see the gift of action, even if sometimes unthinking and impulsive. In the other disciples, the gift of faithfulness and practicality, even if it sometimes seems pedestrian and uninspired. Yet every single gift is needed in that group and in every community that seeks the presence of Christ as Lord.

The first steps away from immobilized sorrow, though they began in failure, have produced a return, in this case the draught of fishes. This investment of energy is met by a further energy, which Christ offers in response. John says, "When they got out on land, they saw a charcoal fire there, with fish lying on it, and bread." When we find even a flicker of energy and expend it, in a strange way, more is generated. We offer ourselves; Christ offers himself. It is not magic, but it is a mystery. A further mystery is that Christ honours our human need to contribute to our own spiritual formation, which he is carrying out. Here by the lake he says to these men, "Bring some of the fish that you have just caught." So Christ, in his dealings with us, calls us to bring our gifts and our insights, however dimmed they are; our energies, however faltering.

Our physical powers play an important part in our sense of who we are. We rejoice in them; certainly Peter did. His instinct is always to take some action. "Simon Peter," says John, "went aboard and hauled the net ashore." In one burst of energy the job is done. There is no messing around with the involvement of others, no time-consuming appeal for participation, no complex giving of assignments, no delegating! We are all aware of this style of doing things. It was Peter's way, most certainly, on this occasion.

Only one thing stands in its way, the method of Christ. In his way we see a readiness to accept the unpredictability and frustration of community involvement. He himself possesses power, insight, wisdom; yet he insists on gathering a community and drawing out our lesser powers, lesser insights, lesser wisdom. Here on the early morning beach, in offering bread and fish, our Lord communicates this to the disciples and to us.

Because of this there is an element in Christ's quiet question to Peter that can easily be missed. Jesus says, "Simon, son of John, do you love me more than these"? It seems as if the two are now on their own, distanced a little from the others. It is almost as if Christ is saying to Peter, "I suspect that you don't feel as great an attachment to these others as you do to me; isn't that right?" I wonder aloud if this implication is in our Lord's question, because when Peter responds, telling of his deep commitment, he is immediately countered by our Lord and directed (even, we might say, redirected) to the task: "Feed my lambs." I wonder if, as the risen Lord said this, he didn't look over in the direction of the nearby group of very ordinary men, whose greasy fingers are handling pieces of fish and whose rough robes wipe the bread crumbs from appreciative lips. I cannot help but feel that our Lord is here admonishing Peter to involve them. Thus our Lord, as we meet him in scripture on this morning beach, admonishes us to involve others, to honor the gifts of others, even if they seem ordinary and limited gifts.

Three times Peter is asked the quiet penetrating question that so unerringly identifies his greatness and his failing. The question is asked so that his gift of independent initiative may become more valuable by recognizing its own limitations. This kind of question threatens us all. It involves self-assessment, accountability, self-criticism. "Peter was grieved because he said to him the third time, 'Do you love me?' "

There is more evidence in our Lord's next words to Peter that he is dealing with something in Peter that is both strength and weakness. There follows a vivid portrait of Peter as he is, relatively young, in his prime. Then there is a flash of the future, an old age of weakness and dependence. It is as if our Lord is still trying to shape Peter for his future tasks, trying to show this fiercely independent man that dependence doesn't necessarily begin only when we can no longer avoid it. It is not a burden to be grudgingly accepted only when inevitable. Dependence, in the sense of our being *interdependent,* is the essence of being human. The acknowledgement of this, far from being failure, is true achievement. Only when we realize this, can we realize whom we follow and toward what personal transformation we are being led. The Lord at this point says to Peter "Follow me."

There follows a moment so totally human that it cannot be other than a personal experience. John may have begun to approach Peter and our Lord. As he comes forward, Peter says very quietly and urgently "What about this man?" It is a strange question, unshaped and spare, as if coming from the instincts rather than thought, spoken before it could be stifled. Was the coming of John seen as a threat to the passionately held relationship that Peter had with the familiar yet awesome figure beside him? Was there the fear that the other very different gifts of John would be accepted before those of Peter? Is there a hint of jealousy, a chronic lack of self-esteem in Peter, which we know so well in ourselves?

One is tempted to suspect this because there is, in our Lord's response, an obvious wish to calm Peter. "If it is my will that he remain until I come, what is that to you? Our Lord seems to be reassuring Peter, and hereby saying to us, that a relationship with Christ as Lord is not necessarily greater or less than the relationships of others with him. A relationship with our Lord is its own measuring rod. It is absolute. As our Lord had to assure his greatest apostle, so he assures us. All we are asked to do is to follow.

The Inn

That very day two of the apostles were going to a village named Emmaus, about seven miles from Jerusalem, and talking with each other about all these things that had happened. While they were talking and discussing together, Jesus himself drew near and went with them. But their eyes were kept from recognizing him. And he said to them, "What is this conversation which you are holding with each other as you walk?" And they stood still, looking sad. Then one of them, named Cleopas, answered him, "Are you the only visitor to Jerusalem who does not know the things that have happened there in these days?" And he said to them, "What things?" And they said to him, "Concerning Jesus of Nazareth, who was a prophet mighty in deed and word before God and all the people. And he said to them, "O foolish men, and slow of heart to believe all that the prophets have spoken! Was it not necessary that the Christ should suffer these things and enter into his glory?" So they drew near to the village to which they were going. He appeared to be going further, but they constrained him, saying, "Stay with us, for it is toward evening and the day is now far spent." So he went in to stay with them. When he was at table with them, he took the bread and blessed, and broke it, and gave it to them. And their eyes were opened and they recognized him; and he vanished out of their sight.

Luke 24:13–19, 25, 26, 28–31

• • •

We speak of something as being "out of sight, out of mind." Sometimes the experience we have had in a certain place, the complexity of feelings we have had to handle, can be dealt with only by flight. Columba, in the long ago brutal yet lovely Celtic Christian dawn, was filled with such self-loathing that his only option was to rig a sail and head out into the

wilderness of the Atlantic. He sailed until eventually he found
an island from which the land of guilt and regret could not even
be seen.

I thought of this in Emmaus. I had stood at the low railings of
the lookout point, and my eyes had followed the arrows
carved into into the low wall for tourists such as me. Yet,
whenever I looked, it was the same — a sea of hills and valleys,
their endless waves of scattered stones white against the brown
of the earth and the tough burnt grasses. After a while I came
back into the grove of trees beside the church, lay down on a
wall, and looked up into the branches. I suppose it would have
taken them nearly three hours to get here from Jerusalem. But
then, of course, the whole point is that they never got here.
The glory of the thing, the joy of it all, is that they never
reached Emmaus. This is the victory. If they had come over the
brow of the hill behind me, they would have been home. But
that would have been a defeat.

Luke is the only one of the evangelists who tells their story.
It is mid-morning on the first day of the week. It is easy for the
Christian memory of imagine an idyllic Sunday morning in
traditional terms. We celebrate the memory of this particular
day always on a Sunday, Easter Day. But, for these men and
women of whom Luke is writing, the first day in the week was
the equivalent of a Monday. The shutters of shops were rattl-
ing upward, the streets of the city were erupting into their
usual smell and noise and turmoil. Sabbath had ended. The
time for dreams was over. The real world was returning.

I think it important to say this, because it may well have
been that eruption of brutal reality which forced at least two
followers of the dead Galilean to wipe the dust of Jerusalem off
their feet. Very frequently, when we ourselves face shattering
bereavement, nothing gives us greater pain than to see life
going on normally around us. We feel like screaming at everybody and everything. Do they not know the unspeakable thing
that has happened? Our friend, our wife, our child, our parent
— whoever it may be — is dead. How can the fabric of life not

come apart, as our deepest being is torn apart? How can it go on as if nothing has happened? Such, I suspect, were the feelings that brought about the decision to go to Emmaus. Why that little village? We can only surmise. Luke names one of the two as Cleopas. We know that one of the women of the early community, named Mary, is identified as the wife of Clopas. It may well be that they were living in Emmaus, or had done so, or had family there.

From Luke we know another significant thing about these two. We know that on this very same day — hours before we meet them at this noon time heading out of Jerusalem — they had been with the rest of the disciples when the women had burst in among them with news of the shattering experience at the tomb of Jesus. Apparently that news had not done anything to dispel their agony. Furthermore, by their own admission, we know they were aware that others had gone to check the tomb and had "found it just as the women had said." Still they registered total loss and shock. In that frame of mind they made their decision — if it was really a decision. We know enough of our own ways of responding to shock to realize that their going could have been a blind unseeing rush from everything associated with the friend whom they had lost so tragically.

"A village named Emmaus . . . seven miles from Jerusalem." Deliberately or not life places us between village and city. It is significant for us that this is precisely the context of our own lives. Much of the contemporary struggle with life in big cities — the tendency to alienate, to create loneliness, anger, sometimes even nervous breakdown — may come from the fact that millions of older adults are rooted in rural villages and small towns. For them the vast city is a later experience in life, which often creates an unrealized nostalgia for the consciously forgotten but deeply remembered village. In city life, especially in times of crisis or difficulty, the psychological village is thought of as just over the shining hills of memory. We see this in many ways — in the story of the senior executive who migrates to the small town, the naming of vast suburban developments with rustic "village" sounding names. In many senses, all of us are drawn out toward the Emmaus road.

The journey to Emmaus takes us, as it took Cleopas and his companion, on a search for simplicity. For them the city had been the place of intense excitement and anticipation. Probably they and others had entered it shouting their ecstatic Hosannas only days before. In the ensuing days the city had become a place first of rejection, then of alarm and danger, finally of horror. In five terrible days the complex forces and institutions of Jerusalem had shattered their most dearly held hopes and broken the deepest relationship they had ever experienced. Now they would look for comfort in the simplicities, real or imagined, of a village world. No wonder they were, as Luke says, "talking with each other about all these things that had happened." What else could there be to talk about? Their universe had collapsed. No wonder that, in their total self-concern, they were oblivious to anything or anybody else.

"While they were talking and discussing together, Jesus himself drew near and went with them." As we ourselves take part in countless conversations, discussions, prayer and Bible study groups, we might savour that simple but profound statement. As we thrash about in our human dialogue — sometimes creative, sometimes frustrating — it is so easy to forget that we have been promised his presence. If our intentions genuinely incline toward deepening our relationship with the risen Christ, then, he has promised us, "Where two or three are gathered in my name, there am I in the midst of them." We know this promise in a cerebral way, just as the two on the Emmaus road knew that something had happened at the tomb. But it had registered only as information — precisely as much of our religious life can, if we so choose, remain as mere information. It does not issue into a knowing that goes beyond information. With the two on the Emmaus road, even meeting someone was no more than a half-observed fact. It was irrelevant to their discussion. Talking about Jesus in endless well-intentioned Christian discussions is often just a memorializing of a past event. Because of this there is in them, and in us, no expectation that Christ is to be encountered in present experience as a living reality. As Luke says, "Their eyes were kept from recognising him."

The Stranger says to them, "What is this conversation which you are holding with each other as you walk?" They stand still, looking sad. Their stance, he implies, is that of resentment. The stranger has intruded on a private agony, and they, as would we, feel that the effort to explain is too much, because nobody will ever be able to understand. It is Cleopas who expresses the resentment, mingled with impatience and sarcasm. He makes it absolutely obvious that they wish this conversation to end as quickly as possible. Sorrow very often makes us reject an offered relationship. Ironically this is the very thing we may need. Cleopas says, "Are you the only visitor to Jerusalem who does not know the things that have happened . . ."

The Stranger does what all sensitive listeners to sorrow do. He creates the opportunity for the reason for sorrow to be told again. He says merely, "What things?" The flood gates open. Luke hardly finds a moment for breath or punctuation in the telling. There is the evocation of the beloved face and name, the revulsion against the perpetrators, the forlorn echo of a great and disappointed hope, the wistful clutching at the straw of the women's news, followed by a dismissal of its possibility. Even to hope is only to court more disappointment and despair.

At that moment the stranger moves from detachment to intensity. While the two in the road are swept forward on their actual journey, they are also taken backward down the highway of their spiritual tradition and its sacred scriptures. A compelling pattern emerges. Pieces of an ancient jig-saw puzzle begin to come together. From the pieces a face begins to emerge. For them it is still a remembered face, last seen twisted and gaunt in death. That awful memory has eradicated any

concept of the living face. They listen entranced as "he interpreted to them in all the scriptures the things concerning
himself."

Before they realized it, "they drew near to the village to
which they were going." Luke gently points to a deep truth. He
says of the Stranger that "he appeared to be going further."
Ironically, the risen Christ had already gone immeasurably
further than these two travellers could ever go. More than
endless miles stood between them. Had they but known it,
they were conversing across two levels of being which we have
no words to analyze or explain.

But they, as we, long for the company of one who can give
meaning to our experience. The invitation is given readily.
That they should invite him to stay is an indication of how
their attitude has already been transformed. Around the table
the questions continue. They must understand, must find the
meaning of what happened. This is a deep instinct in our
bereavement. But the flow of words stops. With simple
deliberation, as if each action is now itself a word, the Stranger
takes bread, blesses, breaks, shares. As action follows action,
the deceptive simplicity assumes a shattering significance.
Their universe explodes in ecstatic recognition. Worlds of
unimaginable possibility swirl about them. Emotions almost
too deep for expression struggle to be released. And as they
emerge from the emotional storm, they realize that they are
alone.

But, very significantly, this time there is no sense of loss.
Instead there is discovery. Someone has not been taken from
them, something has been given and received. The petulance
and depression of the earlier afternoon have gone and given
place to burning excitement. They now realize it started when
the pieces of scripture began to be assembled and a face began
to emerge. "They rose that same hour and returned to
Jerusalem."

Return to the city is made possible by the realization that the
city does not have power of death over truth and faith and

love. When they burst in on the community, they are met with an echo of their own experience. Simon too has encountered a Stranger.

Their experience is ours. First, there is the road from the contemporary city toward which, in our despair, we sometimes turn. There is the attraction of an imagined simplicity which will make survival possible. Maybe it is possible to move from pressure, anxiety, over-stimulation, computerized billing, nuclear holocaust. Maybe in the Emmaus of our dream we will be able to believe again, to hope again. Such is our longing, and in the direction of this longing we sometimes go. As we journey, the Stranger offers us three things. The Stranger, who of course is no stranger, offers us word and sacrament. These things are by way of invitation to return to where we must function. We are men and women of Jerusalem, the city is the reality of our time. This is true strangely enough whether or not we live in a rural area. Today Jerusalem is wherever we can encounter the telephone, the radio, the television, the video cassette recorder, the satellite in the night sky. When we decide to return to Jerusalem, energized by word and sacrament in the inn of our encounter with the risen Christ, we discover his third gift. We discover the community who eat and drink the holy things, who tell the story. In that good company we discover that he is present as risen Lord.

The City

They rose that same hour and returned from Emmanus to Jerusalem; and they found the eleven gathered together and those who were with them, who said, "The Lord has risen indeed, and has appeared to Simon!" Then they told what had happened on the road, and how he was known to them in the breaking of the bread. As they were saying this, Jesus himself stood among them. But they were startled and frightened, and supposed that they saw a spirit. And he said to them, "Why are you troubled, and why do questionings rise in your hearts? See my hands and my feet, that it is I myself; handle me, and see; for a spirit has not flesh and bones as you see that I have." And while they still disbelieved for joy, and wondered, he said to them, "Have you anything here to eat?" They gave him a piece of broiled fish, and he took it and ate before them.

Luke 24:33–43

• • •

Late on Thursday night the prisoner was taken. Some of his friends were in the area when the security detachment arrived, but they fled. Nobody had given orders to pursue them. Official assessment said that without their leader the rest were harmless. In a week they would be back up north at the lake, swearing as they wrestled the huge fish nets into their boats. They of course did not go north immediately. They found their way way back, by various routes, to the city. There is a strong likelihood that they gradually returned to the upper room where they had shared a meal earlier that evening. None of them knew what should be done. Hours went by and Peter did not come; so they assumed he had been taken. Eventually he would return, and they would realize that something terrible had happened. It would take a long time before he would be

·able to tell how he was identified more than once as a friend of the accused, and that he denied it.

What they did do as a group was instinctive. They locked the door, and like frightened animals gone to ground, they licked their emotional wounds. They ate what could be found, and they slept the sleep of exhaustion. Probably at some moment in the pre-dawn hours, Peter came back. We simply do not know what they did on the following day, the Sabbath. They may have emerged carefully, either individually or in pairs. We can be certain that they had no wish to attract attention. By the time the long hours of the day had dragged through, they may have begun making plans for heading home. For most of them home meant Galilee. Generally in all of us there is an instinct to head for home when trouble must be dealt with or endured.

Those plans for the immediate future were drastically shattered in the early hours of the first day of the new week. It began with the mingled sobs and breathlessness of Mary of Magdala blurting out her news. They didn't really believe her. Other women came to tell of a similar experience. It was John who simply could not contain himself any longer. They had all been cooped up for too long. John, propelled by Mary's semi-coherent information, tore out of the room. Peter immediately followed him. When they eventually returned and told what they had found — especially the way the body wrapping had been left collapsed on the low stone shelf — the group knew that something extraordinary was taking place. All the evidence suggests that none of them was remotely prepared to be more specific than that.

We are taken by Luke into that long ago circle of faces. Now with him we are able to follow two figures hurrying back to Jerusalem. They are heading toward the city from the north west, down the Emmaus road. We listen as they tell the group their unbelievable experience. They are bombarded with a thousand questions and made the centre of frantic attention.

There, one by one, at no particular moment but with absolute certainty, they become aware of a new presence among them. "As they were saying this," Luke writes, "Jesus himself stood among them."

In the beleagured upper room of our own century, in a Christianity not quite sure of its place in the world or its relationship with society, there is understandably endless discussion. Curiously enough, it is about the question that engaged them behind locked doors in the upper room. The talk is mainly of the future. What is ahead for the church? What is the future of faith? The talk, now as then, is also about Jesus. The disciples must have spent that first terrible weekend reminiscing, probably indulging in some "if only" talk. If only they had persuaded him not to come south. If only he had not attacked the money exchange booths in the temple. If only.

In a sense, we too talk a great deal about Jesus. The late twentieth century, having inherited sixteen hundred year old Greek thought forms by which to shape and to express its beliefs about Jesus Christ, is now doing a great deal of discussing and writing about the need to find ways of speaking about the mystery of the Incarnation that will engage, attract, and challenge contemporary thought. All of this is invaluable and unavoidable. Every generation, including biblical generations, has had to find ways by which men and women speak to one another about the nature of God. One thing is essential — that while we go through the struggle to articulate, to define, to theologize, we remain aware that the living Christ, who is never going to be made the captive of our thought forms or our word descriptions, is standing daily among us. In the words of Luke, we take note of this fact: "While they were saying this, Jesus himself stood among them."

Their response is also significant for us. "They . . . supposed," says Luke, "that they saw a spirit." The word *spirit* is translated elsewhere as "ghost." They thought they were seeing a ghost. Much Christian belief, unknown to itself, is belief in a ghost. To the degree that Christians are given to thinking of Jesus Christ as in any sense a past reality (a very wonderful past reality, we all hastily add!), to that degree we are believing in a ghost. In so far as we think of Christianity as an admirable philosophy or a highly moral code of conduct, to that degree we are believing in a ghost called Jesus Christ. In so far as we look on sacramental things such as bread and wine as pleasant universal symbols to jog our memories about Jesus, to that degree we are believing in a ghost.

Luke communicates a tone of concern in the words of the risen Christ. Is there a hint of disappointment at their reaction? "Why do questionings arise in your hearts"? It sounds like a loving yet pitying reflection on the human condition by one who knows that condition through and through yet has moved beyond it. Immediately our Lord challenges them at the point of greatest vulnerability in their belief. He emphasizes his own physical reality. "See my hands and my feet that it is I myself; handle me, and see; for a spirit has not flesh and bones as you see that I have."

Today's Christianity finds that it must do now as our Lord did then. Its reality can be commended most effectively in actions, in specific contributions made to an agonized world and a profoundly unjust society. Only thus can the Christian faith show the reality at its heart. To act is to show the world "hands" and "feet."

Three times in the words already quoted our Lord emphasizes his physical reality. Not content even with this emphasis, he asks a question that has a familiar ring, because of the years they have spent together. Our Lord says, "Have you anything here to eat?" It will be said again from a fog-shrouded lakeside beach in Galilee. It is as if our Lord wanted this simple action of eating to provide the ultimate assurance of his reality to that long ago community.

To us in today's communities the words come gradually into our hearing. We kneel or stand with others. At first we hear a distant voice saying the simple but infinitely profound statement over and over again. It becomes more and more distinct as the bearer of sacred wine and bread comes nearer, until for a fleeting moment there exists only oneself and the encountered reality. "The Body of Christ: the bread of heaven. The Blood of Christ; the cup of salvation." This is the physical means of grace which comes to our physical being. Both are the dwelling places of God. Here is encounter. Without this eating and drinking we die.

> Here O my Lord I see thee face to face;
> Here faith touch and handle things unseen.

The lines are one of the few examples of our coming even near to finding words for the mystery of the Eucharist. The writer has captured it in a paradox easily missed as we sing the familiar hymn. He speaks of the moment when we come to "handle things unseen." He has expressed in three words the almost indescribable mingling of realities that is hidden within the sacramental act. Thus does the risen Lord communicate for ever the profound central truth that will characterize the world-wide faith that in the future will flow from this tiny roomful of confused men and women. However that faith will articulate itself in words, it will have at its heart the simple tangible elements of bread and wine. By their simplicity and their universality they will testify to the living reality of the risen Lord, who in these familiar mysteries enters body and soul. Bread and wine bear the king into the citadel of our human lives as surely as the foal of an ass bore him royally, yet with deceiving simplicity, into a long ago Jerusalem.

Among his disciples our Lord now moves from sacrament to word. Luke tells us that "he opened their minds to understand the scriptures." Again this statement has a familiar ring. We heard it only a few hours ago through the ears of the two walking with the Stranger on the road to Emmaus, where "he interpreted to them in all the scripture the things concerning himself."

At the very beginning of the Christian story, even before the new movement has been born in the fire of Pentecost, the risen

Lord offers the second great source of grace for the future. The acting out of sacrament is followed by the emphasis on word. The keeping and telling of a tradition is to be important. Christians are to be people with a story. The first great telling of the story, the old telling or testament, enshrined in the scrolls of synagogue and the sacrifices of temple, is to be seen as pointing to the terror and joy of the Resurrection event now being acted out in this very room. The second or new telling is yet to be written. There is a very strong tradition that the home in which the upper room was situated was that of Mary the mother of the young John Mark. If so, there may well have been, in this very home at this moment, the youth who would tell part of the new story in his writing of what would come to be known as gospel.

Word and sacrament, the two great foundations of all that is to come, have been laid down in this encounter. What remains now is the directive as to how to use them. They are above all to be shared, to be passed on, to be "preached in his name to all nations, beginning at Jerusalem." The events of the gospel, the shared memories of an intimacy with him in the loveliness of Galilee, cannot be kept as private memory. These men and women who "are witnesses of these things" must tell of what they saw and heard and felt. In the relationship with Jesus they caught glimpses of a kingdom, but they cannot occupy it selfishly. Its gates must be opened to others. Our Lord is naming a third great work of the future. To sacrament and word he now adds mission.

How easily that word rolls off the Christian tongue, and how difficult it is to define in this decade. On a personal basis, what is the mission of a Christian? There are Christians for whom the answer is crystal clear and simple. Mission is the bringing of other men and women into a personal relationship with the living Christ. When one has said that, the important question is How. Christians vary in their answers — some claiming the right to confront others directly and challengingly, others wishing merely to communicate their own faith in very quiet implicit ways, some not speaking of the faith at all unless asked specifically about it.

Questions about the individual mission of Christians are further complicated by the demands of a plural society where, in the western world particularly, religion is regarded as a totally personal and subjective element of life. Looming over such questions are the further questions about the mission of the churches. Do churches have a mission to put Christian claims before power structures and institutions in society? Can Christian mission sometimes be a call for criticism and challenge to the essential structures of a country's life? Certainly the prophets of the Old Testament thought so. Many Christians think so, but many do not. When our Lord called those early disciples to mission, he called them into something that would frequently bring them, even in their generation, into conflict with the society they lived in. Mission can be simple and complex, personal and political, rewarding and costly.

Next there comes what is here only a single phrase easily missed. "I send the promise of my Father upon you," our Lord says. It is a hint of the mystery of Pentecost, which is yet to happen. At this moment nothing is made specific. There is no point in explaining something that will not be comprehended, even after it sweeps through them in fire and ecstasy. All that is done now is to make a kind of rendezvous for the event. He says, "Stay in the city, until you are clothed with power from on high." Twenty centuries later we hear that directive with piercing and complex meaning. Our task as Christians, it would seem, is to "stay in the city." That small word *city* means for us a phenomenon that has changed and possessed the world. It means vast urbanization, population explosion, technology, secularization, pluralism. It means the world as our late century knows it.

Sometimes we feel the "city," the "civilized" world, is not only an impossible environment for faith and for faith community, but we feel it is the actual enemy of God and must undergo apocalyptic destruction to be cleansed and transformed. Political radicalism (which is a kind of an apocalyptic) claims that the city can be transformed within history. Religious radicalism, in its various forums of fundamentalism, and millenarianism, claims that the city will be transformed by the divine initiative but that the transformation will take place beyond history. We are in a complex domain, which has been and will always be the stuff of theological discussion. Here in the encounter with his disciples, the risen Lord says two things that are necessary to hear again as we struggle with the place of faith in the urban technical world. He says, "Stay in the city," and adds, "until you are clothed with power from on high." If we are prepared to believe that what is said by the risen Lord to that community then is also said timelessly to the Christian community now, it should serve us as a contemporary grace. If the promise of Christ is that power and grace can be found in urban civilization, then that promise is itself grace. It enables us to live faithfully in the midst of the city of our time.

The Highway

Now as Saul journeyed he approached Damascus, and suddenly a light from heaven flashed about him. And he fell to the ground and heard a voice saying to him, "Saul, Saul, why do you persecute me?" And he said, "Who are you, Lord?" And he said, "I am Jesus, whom you are persecuting; but rise and enter the city, and you will be told what you are to do." The men who were traveling with him stood speechless, hearing the voice but seeing no one. Saul arose from the ground; and when his eyes were opened, he could see nothing; so they led him by the hand and brought him into Damascus. And for three days he was without sight, and neither ate nor drank. Acts 9:3–9

• • •

We meet Saul of Tarsus for the first time at the scene of a public execution. He is not himself taking part in the awful process, but he has been involved in the decision to carry out the sentence. Luke, as he writes the Acts of the Apostles, makes this perfectly clear. "Saul," he writes, "was consenting to his [Stephen's] death."

One is highly unlikely to view a public execution, especially as prolonged and brutal as a public stoning, without it remaining in the memory. Perhaps Saul was even more likely to remember Stephen's death since they were approximately the same age, each had a brilliant mind, each was highly articulate, each was fiercely loyal to his own faith. Luke seems to be hinting at a certain struggle going on in Saul when he tells us that soon after the execution, when a persecution of the new faith began, "Saul was ravaging the church, and entering house after house, he dragged off men and women and committed them to prison." Saul would not be the first or last to try to quieten inner conflict by frantic and obsessive activity.

We encounter Saul on the road that comes out of the highlands between Israel and Syria. When we do meet him, we are immediately aware of a mood. Luke writes, "But Saul, still breathing threats and murder against the disciples of the Lord, went to the high priest and asked him for letters to the synagogues at Damascus, so that if he found any belonging to the Way, men or women, he might bring them bound to Jerusalem." Even the style of the writing creates an atmosphere. That long sentence setting the scene hardly allows one to pause for breath. It begins in the seething depths of Saul himself and hurtles on ahead to our destination in Damascus. It flashes before us the faces of the small Christian community, doubles back to the cold authority of Jerusalem, and menacingly reaches out as if to eradicate a potential threat to social and religious conformity.

The threatened community is called the *Way*. A lovely and gentle word! It was the great, perhaps unwitting, compliment paid by their contemporaries to those first followers of Jesus. They seemed to others to have found an intriguing and attractive Way to live. It did not, of course, attract everybody. Saul's determination to root it out is evidence of that. But those who were drawn to it, felt that this new Way of personal and community life gave meaning to existence. It seemed to embrace a fully human way of life yet to possess and to give a kind of grace and hope which transcended that humanity. There was a reason for a significant community of Christians being in Damascus. Already attitudes for and against the Way were hardening, especially in and around Jerusalem. Many who had become identified with Jesus of Nazareth found it expedient to seek the cosmopolitanism and greater tolerance of the more northerly cities in Syria, especially Damascus and Antioch.

Many times in the future the amazing story would be told. Saul himself, later to be known as Paul, would tell it again and again, almost as if the trauma had seared his memory. We hear him years later, in the middle of a wild mob he has managed to quieten so that he can be heard. "As I made my journey and drew near to Damascus, about noon a great light from heaven suddenly shone about me. And I fell to the ground" (Acts 22:6).

The one who a moment ago is the focus of everything, who radiates authority and power, is sprawling on the roadway, instinctively scrambling in the dust to avoid the hoofs of the startled horse. At the same time he is engaged in another struggle not so obvious, impossible for his horrified companions to understand. Afterward they will recall a light, a kind of flash, gone before it can fully be perceived. They will recall that Saul seems almost oblivious of them. There seems for him to be someone else. They hear Saul's whispers, groping words being formed. They watch him gazing into the searing sunlight as if unaware of its danger, almost as if he were trying to penetrate its terrible blaze to see something beyond vision. Paul will often try passionately to explain what had been happening in those moments. It seems each time as if he despairs of communicating the depth of what he had experienced.

There is a peculiar terror when something threatening affects us while travelling. In unfamiliar circumstances it is essential to have our wits about us. Even a minor pain or nausea felt in the teeming solitariness of a distant airport or hotel can be disproportionately chilling. We feel we must remain in charge; we simply have to exert our energy and focus our faculties. There are duties to perform, decisions to be made, appointments to be kept.

So it was on that long ago Damascus Road. For a highly motivated and formidably able man, there certainly were appointments to be kept and tasks — unpleasant tasks — to be completed. Suddenly power is taken from him and passes to something or Someone else. As he falls, his dignity is ripped away. His deepest self-esteem is devastated. Somehow he cannot even see things. Total fear grips him. "He fell to the ground and heard a voice saying to him, 'Saul, Saul, Why do you persecute me?' "

It is strange how frequently the losing of power and control releases us to question and be questioned. The terror of a heart attack, the sense of everything slipping, the helplessness felt, can eventually lead to questions from oneself or from others, an asking Why of many things. Why do we act in a certain way? Why have certain habits and attitudes formed? Why is there anger or anxiety or hatred? So it is with Saul. Someone, in this case the risen Christ, asks him the devastating question, Why. It is, of course, the one question that both Paul and we rarely pause to ask. There is in him an obsession to destroy something. Obsession, anger, hatred, never ask Why. Yet the moment this question can be asked, there is the possibility of great change.

"Why do you persecute me?" says the voice. The question focuses on a person. This can have a transforming effect on our attitudes. Causes, movements, programs, ideas — all are impersonal. We so easily adopt stances to them. If we choose to, we can hate them, approve them, attack them, condemn them. But let anyone of them encounter us in a person, and we have to think again. To Saul, an idea, a movement, has become suddenly a person. That person speaks from the depths of Saul's own being, for that is where the person has come to dwell. In persecuting this person, Saul persecutes the deepest part of himself.

Saul now asks a question. "Who are you, Lord?" Even as he does so, he answers himself with the word that is wrung from him, *Lord*. Saul, a man of power, recognizes a greater power; his instinct for authority feels a vaster authority all around him. There is not yet full recognition of Him who has initiated this encounter. But depths that Saul has never probed before give up what he has long submerged with passionate intensity. The name his conscious mind has set out to eliminate resonates within him. He is consumed by a new compulsion, but this one is intoxicatingly liberating. The memory of it will in the future make him protest that all his many-faceted gifts and insights are "no longer I . . . but Christ who lives in me." This experience will have him speak of himself as "a servant of Christ."

There is however a revealing paradox. In this fierce and blazing moment of self-illumination, when Saul has come spiritually to discern so much, he is physically blind. It would seem as if he must be blinded so that he can be shown another way. He must submit to another will so that his own will may find its true direction. Here is the essence of all true spirituality, to be learned both by those of us who stagger as spiritual infants in the outer courts of the Lord, and by those great ones who sit at the tables of heaven.

"Rise and enter the city," Saul is told. But how differently does he enter and for how different a purpose than his original intent! He who would have come to this city brandishing his delegated power now totters in under its great gate "led . . . by the hand." We all go into the city. We go daily. We go for pleasure or for work. We go gladly or sullenly, fearfully or with fascination. We may bring authority, competence, creativity, power, as we take our morning journey to the city. But whose power do we really acknowledge? How wise are we, really? To what extent are we aware of our limitations, our blindness to so much of what Christ would have us see — such things as poverty, need, injustice?

In such fashion did Saul come to Damascus. In a sense, he never reached the city. Saul left Jerusalem, but Paul stumbled into Damascus. Saul could see and yet was lost. Paul was blind but had been found. Indeed Paul had found, and had been found by, Christ. Luke tells us that "for three days he was without sight, and neither ate nor drank." As with Christ in the tomb, so it was with Saul in his darkness. So it is with us all. There is a divine pattern here. We have acted out this pattern in retreat; we have acted it out in quiet, in suffering, in betrayal and disappointment. We have all known the tomb, the darkness so impenetrable that we can see nothing inside or beyond ourselves.

But in our "Damascus" experiences there also is one whose foot steps approach. For Saul it is a local Christian named Ananias. The one who approaches comes to roll the stone from our frequently self-constucted tomb, to open the door of our desperately locked room. The voice of Ananias says simply, "Brother Saul," and Luke tells us, "Immediately something like scales fell from his eyes." Likewise, at dark times for us someone has come and touched us in love. It matters not who it is. What matters is that they were, and always will be, sent. When we feel their touch we, like Saul, rise healed and energized for the new tasks to which we are called.